Intermediate 2
Sport & Recreation

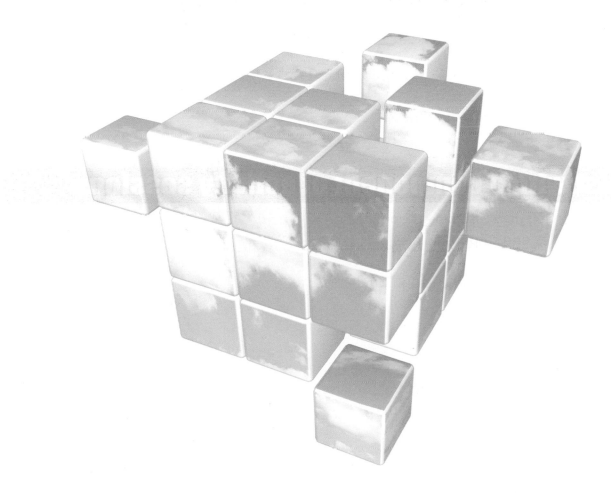

× Emma Hayes ×

Contents

Introduction

Assist with fitness programming

Assist with a component of activity sessions

Assist with daily centre duties

Employment opportunities in the sport and recreation industry

Glossary and index

Guide to symbols

(symbol with 6)	Whenever you see this symbol, it highlights where you will cover an employability skill. This is indicated by the number in its centre (see page 9 for a list of employability skills).
(Top Tip symbol)	These stars give you TOP TIPS on what you need to revise or learn on each page.
(Quick test symbol)	At the end of each section there are QUICK TESTS to test your knowledge.

Foreword

The Skills for Work courses are designed to allow you to experience the World of work. This may be achieved by you having access to realistic Sport and Recreation environments in a variety of both indoor and outdoor settings. You will also be encouraged to work with real clients and staff in these different realistic environments. This guide will help you prepare for this exciting, but challenging, World of Work as it prepares you to complete assessments in a realistic environment rather than conventional classroom settings.

This Success Guide covers each of the five mandatory units in the Intermediate 1 Sport & Recreation course. One topic area is addressed per double page spread to help you manage your progress through the course. While you are working through the course, it will allow you to gain an insight into what is involved when working in Sport and Recreation facilities, such as, leisure centres, outdoor centres, fitness gyms and swimming pools, etc.

This book aims to support that experience and reinforce your learning. Throughout the book, employability skills and self review sections will help you to develop good practice both within and away from the learning environment. This book also provides information on important Health & Safety legislation that you will be required to know for your course.

Bob Nielson
Qualifications Development Manager

What is a 'Skills for Work' course?

The Skills for Work course is designed to help candidates to acquire the necessary skills and knowledge in a particular subject.

In Skills for Work– Sport and Recreation (Intermediate 2), candidates will be supervised at all times by the 'person responsible' while they carry out a range of tasks in a sporting environment. These will be:

- **Assisting with fitness programming**
  Plan, implement and review a client's fitness programme
- **Assisting with a component of activity sessions**
  Plan, assist and review activity sessions; carrying out emergency procedures
- **Assisting with daily centre duties**
  Set up, take down and store equipment; cleaning and tidying facility areas
- **Employment opportunities in the sport and recreation environment**
  Career pathways; identifying skills, qualifications and experience; producing a career plan

Throughout the course, candidates will carry out a range of tasks laid out by the Scottish Qualifications Authority (SQA), called the **Unit Specifications**. These Units are comprehensive documents giving details about what teachers, tutors, trainers, and so on, must do and cover for candidates to pass the course.

Candidates will gain good foundation knowledge and have the basic skills in sport and recreation. This will give candidates a helping hand in furthering their career in this industry, whether they wish to continue in education or to gain employment.

The Skills for Work course is designed to be delivered in a sport and recreation environment and is not suitable for a conventional classroom setting. There are no set environments where the course can be delivered; but here are some examples:

- Sports hall
- Swimming pool
- Gym
- Outdoor centre
- Leisure centre

What are the Skills for Work units?

The Skills for Work – Sport and Recreation (Intermediate 2) course comprises four Units. These Units are designed to give candidates a 'snapshot' of the different duties and activities that employees in the sport and recreation industry carry out on a daily basis.

As mentioned the opposite page, the candidate will be assisting the **person responsible** at all times.

Assist with fitness programming

Candidates gain the opportunity to work with a client to develop a physical training plan with the person responsible. They will identify two components of fitness for the candidates to plan, organise, monitor and review in the client's physical training plan based on the client's fitness baseline test. Candidates will review the client's progress and review their performance with the person responsible.

Assist with a component of activity sessions

Candidates learn what goes into the planning of a component within an activity that the candidate will explain and demonstrate to the participants. Candidates have to identify what equipment they should need, carry out a basic risk assessment and have the plan approved by the person responsible. Candidates will be expected to assist the person responsible with client reviews and a review of their own performance. This Unit also focuses on how emergency procedures are carried out in the sport and recreation setting; and candidates will be expected to carry out these procedures to the level of their responsibility.

Assist with daily centre duties

Candidates work alongside the person responsible to assist with the setting up, taking down and storage of equipment according to centre and manufacturers' guidelines. Candidates will also be supervised in the cleaning and tidying of facility areas and adhering to health and safety guidelines for cleaning materials and equipment. Candidates are expected to assist and respond to client needs.

Employment opportunities in the sport and recreation industry

This Unit covers the basic requirements of industry skills, qualifications and experience. It will allow candidates to understand what they will need to gain in order to progress into employment and to map these requirements against the skills, qualifications and experience they already have. Candidates will then develop a personal career plan based on their mapping exercise.

Training and assessment

This book refers throughout to the 'person responsible'. This person is someone who has direct responsibility for the assigned task and is in a supervisory capacity over the candidate – for example, a teacher/tutor or a coach/instructor.

Most of the Units are designed to be assessed not in a classroom setting but in a 'realistic working environment'. A realistic environment is a facility that allows candidates access to sport and recreation equipment, facilities and clients (customer/users) – for example, a leisure centre, swimming pool, outdoor centre or fitness suites. The Units do allow for aspects of candidates' **training** to be carried out in a **classroom setting** – for example, when teaching the Knowledge and Understanding aspects of dealing with accidents and emergencies; but the **assessments** have to be carried out in a **realistic working environment**.

Although the Units can be taught and assessed separately, the Units within the course were designed to be integrated with each other. An example of this is:

- **Assist with a component of activity sessions and Assist with daily centre duties**: setting up equipment, carrying out an activity session, taking down and storing equipment after use

Candidates are assessed mainly by observation as to whether they can carry out the assigned tasks as listed in the Units. The course allows the candidates to gather equivalent assessment material from their realistic working environment – for example, faulty equipment reports. Candidates will be assessed by a variety of methods, including:

- practical **scenarios**
- assessment by observation
- Knowledge and Understanding set questions
- set proforma assessment papers, such as activity session plans, or accident/ emergency reports
- candidate log sheets

To assist candidates further with their learning, the SFEU (Scottish Further Education Unit) has produced support material to assist teachers, tutors and trainers with the delivery of the Skills for Work – Sport and Recreation course.

What are 'employability skills'?

Key features

A key feature of the Skills for Work course is the **employability skills** that are built into the course. Through undertaking a range of activities and tasks, candidates also work to develop particular skills that are required in the day-to-day lives of the people who work in the sport and recreation industry and these skills are seen by employers as 'necessary' to be able to carry out a variety of jobs in a centre or organisation.

On the opposite page is a table that lists all the employability skills that candidates are assessed on while they are completing Units. During their training candidates will focus on specific employability skills which focus on a particular subject, for example, employability skill number 8 - Timekeeping. Most candidates have had experience in timekeeping:

- Being on time for a bus
- Being on time to meet friends

In each unit, candidates can be given the opportunity to review their employability skills with the person responsible. The candidate have to rate their performance (1 = being very good at that skill/attitude, 5 = being poor), against a list of employability skills that are specific to the Unit they are working on. The person responsible is allowed to give their rating before they review the candidates' performance and listing action points for future training and development.

Employability skills profile

Below is the Scottish Qualifications Authority's Employability Skills Profile. The table shows all the employability skills that can be assessed in all the Units of the Skills for Work course. In the first column are all the employability skills. In the second column are the Units in which these can be found.

A = Sport and Recreation: Assisting with fitness programming

B = Sport and Recreation: Assisting with a component of activity sessions

C = Sport and Recreation: Assisting with daily centre duties

D = Sport and Recreation: Employment opportunities in the sport and recreation industry

Employability Skills	Assessed in Unit
1. Working cooperatively with others	A
2. Review and self-evaluation	B, D
3. Reviewing progress of others	A
4. Setting targets for self and others	A, B, D
5. Positive attitude to learning	B, D
6. Planning and preparation	A, B
7. Customer care/dealing with clients	A, B
8. Time keeping	B
9. Taking advice from others	A, B
10. Wearing appropriate dress	B
11. Giving advice and feedback to others	A, B
12. Awareness of health and safety issues	A, B, C
13. Time management	C

Throughout this book you will be able to find out where the employability skills have been covered by the following symbol. The number contained in the whistle indicates which employability skill has been covered.

Health and safety

Generic health and safety issues

Candidates must be made aware of **basic health and safety** issues that are related to the Units in the Skills for Work – Sport and Recreation course.

Candidates should take part in some form of induction to the course and in the **realistic working environment** where they will be carrying out the tasks detailed in each of the Units.

Each Unit will have its own specific health and safety issues, for example:

Assist with a component of activity sessions:

- Specific activity and equipment safety
- Participant safety
- Risk assessing
- Emergency procedures

Assist with daily centre duties:

- Control of substances
- Personal protective equipment
- Manual handling

Candidates' role within the Skills for Work programme

The Skills for Work course allows candidates to 'learn through practical experience'. It is important to understand what kind of role the candidates will play. The candidates' role, while they are undertaking any tasks, is one that assists the person responsible at all times. At no time should candidates be allowed to take charge of an activity or task without supervision. For more specific information about what tasks the candidates will be assisting with, please refer to the individual Units.

Sport and recreation contacts

For further information and reading:

Organisation's name	Scottish Qualifications Authority	SkillsActive
Address	The Optima Building 58 Robertson Street Glasgow G2 8DQ	Castlewood House 77–91 New Oxford Street London WC1A 1PX
Telephone Number	0845 279 1000	020 7632 2000
Web Site Address	www.sqa.org.uk	www.skillsactive.com
Who are they?	The qualifications authority for Scotland	The Sector Skills Council for Sport and Recreation
Organisation Name	Scottish Further Education Unit	Health and Safety Executive
Address	Argyll Court Castle Business Park Stirling FK9 4TY	HSE Infoline Caerphilly Business Park Caerphilly CF83 3GG
Telephone Number	01786 892000	0845 345 0055
Web Site Address	www.sfeu.ac.uk	www.hse.gov.uk
Who are they?	SFEU is the key development agency for Scotland's colleges.	Responsible for health and safety regulation in Great Britain

Other useful contacts:		
	First aid	STA – www.sta.co.uk BASP – www.basp.org.uk Red Cross – www.redcross.org.uk St John's Ambulance – www.sja.org.uk
	Coaching	Sports leaders – www.bst.org.uk Sportscotland – www.sportscotland.org.uk BWLA – www.bwla.co.uk Lifesavers – www.lifesafers.org.uk
	Other health and safety	BICSc – www.bics.org.uk Child protection – www.childprotectioninsport.co.uk Data protection – http://www.opsi.gov.uk/ACTS/acts1998/19980029.htm

What is fitness programming about?

The practical aspect of this Unit is straightforward; however, there is a certain amount of knowledge that you will need to be taught or will need to revise, to complete this course. If you have completed the Skills for Work – Sport and Recreation (Intermediate 1) Unit *personal fitness*, you will already have a good knowledge base of aspects of fitness. If you have not completed the Intermediate 1 course, your course tutor will be able to go over the important aspects that will cover the points below as part of your Intermediate 2 course.

- The importance of ongoing fitness training and how it is crucial in the development of self and others
- What the components of fitness are
- What a fitness baseline is
- The different types of fitness assessment
- Why plans are drawn up and reviews take place at regular intervals
- The relevant **health and safety** considerations
- How to carry out fitness baseline tests and record results
- Carrying out periodic reviews and making amendments to the plan
- Reviewing results

This Unit is designed for you to learn the basics of fitness programming for a client. It is important that, while you are undertaking any aspects of this Unit, when you carry out tasks they are done under the supervision of the **person responsible** at all times.

With the assistance of the **person responsible**, you will learn how to develop, plan and design a physical training plan for a client. When you meet with the client, you will be completing a PARQ (Physical Activity Record Questionnaire) which will allow you to identify any health issues and understand why the client has chosen to engage in physical activity. It will give you an overall picture of where the client currently is with their fitness level. Once this meeting has finished, it will give you and the person responsible a good overview of the client's aims and objectives and therefore will enable you to set goals.

In this Unit, the client will carry out a fitness baseline test (conducted by you and the person responsible), ensuring that their results are recorded. These results will then help you to choose which two components of fitness are to be chosen in order to help the client meet their objectives, and then you will be expected to plan and design a physical training plan. When designing the plan, it will be important that you take into account any relevant health and safety considerations that may affect the client while they undertake their training.

At regular intervals, you will monitor the client's progress and make any modifications to the original plan along the way. Once the physical training has come to an end, you will then reassess the two components of fitness and again record the results.

When the training period has come to an end you will then (with the person responsible) carry out a review with the client about their physical training, noting down the positive and negative aspects of the plan and their training. You will then take part in a review with the person responsible to identify improvements and make any necessary modifications to the client's plan.

Employability skills in this Unit

In this Unit you will have the opportunity to develop a range of **employability skills**. These are:

1   Working co-operatively with others

3   Reviewing progress of others

4   Setting targets for self and others

6   Planning and preparation

7   Customer care/dealing with clients

9   Taking advice from others

11   Giving advice and feedback to others

12   Awareness of health and safety issues

Top Tip
Look out for the symbol to see where the **employability skills** have been covered.

Top Tip
Remember, any words in GREEN are explained in the GLOSSARY section on pages 94–95.

Components of fitness, and using these when training

It is important to this course that you learn what the different components of fitness are. With the **person responsible**, you will be discussing with the client their overall goals. This will ultimately lead onto which two components of fitness the client will want to improve upon to achieve their goals.

Before taking part in any fitness training, it is important that the advice of the person responsible is sought beforehand because the training may otherwise be harmful to you or to the client.

The components are: flexibility, speed, local muscle endurance, balance, power, cardio-respiratory, strength and agility. Knowledge of these components will help you to improve your client's fitness, which will improve their performance in sporting activities.

The components of fitness

Flexibility

This is the ability to extend the range of motion around a joint or group of joints. The two types of flexibility are:

- Dynamic – when you need flexibility for a short period of time during your overall performance: for example, goalkeepers in hockey only need to perform when they need to defend the goal.
- Static – when you require flexibility for a long period of time: for example, when gymnasts are performing a routine.

Flexibility is required in all sports, as it will reduce the chances of injury (for example, straining or pulling a muscle) and will therefore prepare the muscles for use in exercise. Flexibility exercise should be used appropriately, as it can be detrimental to the body.

To improve flexibility, try: touching your toes; swimming.

Speed

This is the ability to perform a movement in a short period of time. This component may be linked to another (for example, muscle endurance) to achieve your goal. Speed may also be linked to technique and can be crucial to most performance sports, such as:

- Team sports (e.g. football) – where you need speed to avoid a member of the opposing team's tackle.
- Individual sports (e.g. tennis) – where you need speed to return the ball.

To improve your speed, try: running or swimming at a higher speed. However, technique will have to be improved in some sports as well.

Local muscle endurance

This is the ability of the muscle to exert force during an activity and to perform over a long period of time. To improve on this component, you will need to work on the necessary muscle groups with the repetition and intensity in relation to the activity you wish to improve on. For example, a training plan for a kayaker will be different to that for a badminton player.

To improve local muscle endurance, try: rowing; lifting weights; quickly walking or running up stairs.

Balance

This is the ability to control the body's position while moving (dynamic balance) or while in a stationary position (static balance). This may also be part of another component of fitness, such as agility. Examples in sport could be:

Dynamic Balance:

- Skiing – balance is crucial to this sport, as the terrain the skier is travelling over changes continuously, and the skier will need to adapt and keep their balance.

Static Balance:

- Shot-putter – they will have to ensure they are balanced before and after they putt the shot. Without this balance, they may fall over or stumble out of the throwing-circle area.

- Yoga – balance is essential, as the positions require the individual to perform a range of movements and to balance using different parts of the body.

Top Tip
Remember that a slow, gradual approach to training is important; this is done by slowly increasing the amount of repetitions, duration and/or weight over a period of time.

Top Tip
Can you identify the components of fitness? Learn what each component is and how it will affect the client's training.

Quick Test

1. How many components of fitness will you be focusing on?

2. From whom would you be seeking advice when choosing the components of fitness?

3. Name two types of flexibility.

4. Name two types of balance.

Answers 1. Two. **2.** The person responsible. **3.** Dynamic and static. **4.** Dynamic and static.

The components of fitness (cont.)

Power

This is the rate at which we perform work, by exerting great force of strength and speed in an explosive burst of movements. This is measured on how much energy is created, the size of the force applied and the **velocity** with which it is applied.

Power is important in sports that need an explosive reaction, such as a kayaker on the river; they will need speed and strength to negotiate their way around and down the river and will use explosive power to reach their desired location on the river or to get out of a potentially dangerous situation. Another example in sport would be a long jumper; they will need speed to run and strength to take off for the jump.

To improve your power, try: jumping or sprint starting.

Cardio-respiratory

When you take part in cardio-respiratory exercise, it means that your body will need to get the heart to deliver blood to the working muscles over a period of time and to get the lungs to deliver oxygen to the working muscles via the blood supply. What your goals are (for example, to run long distances or to run faster over 100 metres) will determine whether the activity is aerobic or anaerobic:

- Aerobic exercise is where a lot of oxygen is needed to supply the muscles to allow you to work over a longer period of time. These types of activities enable the heart rate to increase, which means the heart will need to work harder and therefore become stronger and be able to work more efficiently. To improve on this type of exercise, try swimming, running or walking for at least 20 minutes a day

- Anaerobic exercise occurs when there is a shortage of oxygen to the muscles, therefore you will need to work for a shorter period of time with a higher level of intensity. To improve on this type of exercise, try: swimming, running or cycling at very high for less than two minutes.

Strength

This is the force the muscles or muscle group can produce. In order to improve on our strength, the muscle will need to be worked beyond its normal operation. Strength is in three categories: dynamic, static and explosive.

- Dynamic – where an athlete's strength is needed to propel them over a distance that may take up to two minutes, for example a 100 metre run.

- Static – where an athlete's strength is needed to hold something in place, such as a position in a rugby scrum.

- Explosive strength is needed by an athlete when they have to perform a single action, such as a movement to reach a distant rock-climbing hold where momentum is required to propel the body.

To improve strength, try: lifting weights; resistance bands/tubes; bodyweight activities.

Agility

This is the ability to carry out a series of power movements quickly in different directions, in an effective and efficient manner. Agility will consist of a combination of other components – balance, speed and strength. Examples in sport would be:

- Tennis – agility is used to return the ball: speed to get to the ball, balance to prevent yourself from slipping or falling as you hit the ball, and strength to hit the ball and return it to the other player.

- Gymnastics – agility is used when gymnasts are carrying out their performance: balance to hold themselves in a position, speed when they are working up to a somersault, and strength to move from a backwards roll into a hand-stand (for example).

To improve agility, try: zigzag running, or breaking down actions/ exercises and repeating them.

Top Tip
Make sure you understand what the components of fitness are.

Top Tip
Learn the different aspects of strength, cardio-respiratory, balance and flexibility, as it will help you to choose the correct training exercises that best suit the client's goals.

Quick Test

1. Name three types of strength exercise.

2. Name two types of cardio-respiratory exercise.

3. What does cardio-respiratory mean?

4. What does velocity mean?

Answers **1.** Dynamic, static and explosive. **2.** Aerobic and anaerobic. **3.** Relating to the heart and lungs. **4.** Measurement of distance travelled per unit of time.

Why do we use the components of fitness?

Different components of fitness

Focusing on different components of fitness and training in the components will help you to improve and perform at a more proficient level during activities. It is important to ensure that the training you give your client is relevant to the sport and to the client's needs.

If, for example, your sport is football, you may want to improve your ability to run for longer. Therefore you will need to focus on your cardio-respiratory exercises.

Below are examples of how to focus on a specific component of fitness and how it can help the client to improve their performance in a sport.

1. To explain this in more detail, we need to identify some different sports.

2. Which components of fitness would help a client improve their performance in these sports?

You will first need to find out what the client is able to do, and whether it is relevant to that sport. For example, the main focus for a rock-climber could be to improve on their ability to climb more difficult routes and hold onto smaller holds, therefore the best component to work on would be strength.

Cardio–respiratory

Improving this component will allow you to increase your play without stopping

Flexibility

Focusing on this component will help you to increase your flexibility range and improve your routine

Strength

Improving on this will help you to improve your ability to climb for longer and on more difficult routes

Muscular endurance

Improving this component will allow you to carry out repetitive activities over a longer time

3. Finally, what kind of exercises would each client need to work on, based on the components of fitness that were identified earlier?

As there are many different kinds of exercises that clients may take part in to improve their performance, the **person responsible** will be able to assist you to choose the most appropriate exercise for the sport or activity. Below are examples of what could be used to improve a client's fitness:

Cardio-respiratory

Clients would carry out at least three 20-minute sessions of continuous activity in a week; these could be jogging, swimming or cycling. By carrying out this kind of training, it will benefit you and the client:

- It will help the client's aerobic capacity
- Easy training programme to follow
- Easy to increase the training time progressively each session
- This kind of training can be carried out without the need for specialist equipment.

Flexibility

To achieve any progression, clients will need to carry out at least 10-12 minutes of stretching exercises daily. These exercises are to be performed slowly (without a bouncing motion). By carrying out this kind of training, it will benefit you and the client:

- Easy to increase the training time progressively each session
- The client will benefit from an increase in flexibility as the training sessions progress
- This kind of training can be carried out without the need for specialist equipment.

Strength

Clients will need to carry out at least two 20-minute sessions a week to improve on their strength. When planning for this type of training, you may have to ensure that the client has access to the appropriate gym facilities. These exercises could include lifting weights. You and the clients will benefit:

- Easy to increase the training time progressively each session
- Allows the client to use equipment to aid their progression.

Muscular endurance

Clients will need to carry out at least three 30-minute sessions a week; these could be exercises that include sit-ups, pull-ups or circuit training. This will benefit you and the client:

- Exercises can be carried out either indoors or outdoors
- Easy to increase the training time progressively each session
- Exercises do not necessarily need complex pieces of equipment.

Top Tip
Make sure the client's needs are taken into account when choosing the two components of fitness for their physical training plan.

Top Tip
Ask the person responsible about the different exercises for each component you will plan for the client.

Quick Test

1. Why will focusing on different components help you improve?

2. How will flexibility help you improve your performance?

3. Name two examples of cardio-respiratory exercises.

4. Name two examples of muscular endurance exercises.

Answers 1. You will perform at a more proficient level. **2.** By increasing your range of motion around a joint or group of joints. **3.** Jogging, swimming or cycling. **4.** sit-ups, pull-ups, circuit training, and so on.

Health and safety

Before preparing and planning a fitness programme for a client, it is vital that you consider the basic aspects of **health and safety** for the client and the environment in which they will be carrying out their training. Each centre will have its own policy documents on health and safety. This will be related to the type of activities and equipment the centre has, and will also inform you of who will be able to use them.

When planning a client's fitness programme, you will need to incorporate the relevant health and safety factors. Some of these factors may relate to:

- The client – are they able to carry out the physical training, or will you need to modify it?
- The environment – where will the client be carrying out the training. Will you need permission to carry out training in a specific venue?

It is important that you consider the points below:

- Make sure you are supervised by the **person responsible** when you are carrying out your fitness programming for a client.
- Ensure that the client has not eaten a large meal before exercising and that they are kept hydrated at all times.
- Ensure that the client is fit and well to carry out any physical exercise and that any needs the client has are addressed at the beginning and at any point during the physical training programme.
- Make sure that you and the client are wearing appropriate clothing and footwear.
- Do warm-up exercises before doing any training and cool-down exercises after you have finished.
- Always follow the manufacturers' guidelines when using any fitness training equipment, and make sure it is in good working condition before using it.
- If you are using a fitness facility, always conduct yourself in an appropriate manner.
- Consider your safety and the safety of the client if you are not using a fitness facility – for example, road running.

Warming up and cooling down

What is it and why do we do it?

The main reason we warm up before doing any activity and cool down afterwards is to get the body ready for exercise.

Warming up takes place before you carry out any exercise, and will:

- reduce the risk of injury.
- increase heart rate and increase blood flow to the muscles – cardio-respiratory exercise (that involves the heart and lungs, such as light running/jogging) which increases to warm the body up.
- allow greater flexibility in joints and muscles (e.g. stretching exercises to muscle groups which will be used during the activity).
- prepare the body and mind for your exercise session.

Cooling down takes place after you have finished your exercise session, and will:

- reduce the risk of muscle soreness or injury. Exercises such as light running/jogging will enable the blood to circulate more oxygen to the muscles, reducing muscle stiffness, and will cool the body down.
- brings the body back to normal gradually. Exercises such as stretching and relaxation exercises will help to bring the body back to its steady state.

You should try to warm up and cool down the relevant muscles for the activity you will be taking part in. The main differences between warm-up and cool-down activities are the length of time you do them for and their intensity. Examples of these exercises for sporting activities could include:

- swimmers: several leisurely laps of the pool
- footballers: shorter sprints at a slower speed
- runners: beginning the run at a slower speed
- tennis: returning the ball to the other player.

Top Tip
Ask the person responsible for examples of the different types of warm-up and cool-down exercises.

Top Tip
Ensure the relevant health and safety aspects are tailored to the physical training plan and the client's needs.

Quick Test

1. When identifying health and safety for the physical training plan, what factors will you have to consider?
2. Who will you be supervised by at all times?
3. Why do we warm up?
4. Why do we cool down?

Answers 1. The client and the environment. **2.** The person responsible. **3.** To get the body ready for exercise. **4.** To bring the body back to normal gradually.

Preliminary consultations

What is a PARQ?

In most centres, before a client takes part in any form of physical training, they undertake some kind of induction where they are asked questions about why they want to take part in training, whether they have any medical issues, and so on. Generally, this is called a 'Physical Activity Record Questionnaire' (PARQ).

The PARQ is designed to formalise the client's induction into the fitness facility and to give you an idea of the client's current lifestyle and why they want to carry out physical activities. Some clients may have medical issues and may have been referred to the centre by a doctor. By gaining this information, you can ensure that the appropriate **health and safety** factors have been highlighted and can ensure the safety of the client.

With the person responsible, you will brief the client on the completion of the PARQ. The brief should include what aspects of the form they will need to complete, and that the rest of the form will consist of a chat or consultation about what their overall goals are and the reasons why they are taking part in a physical training programme.

The first part of the PARQ will be completed by the client, who will complete a 'yes/no' section on their health and medical background. This will show you and the person responsible whether the client is on medication or has any medical problems that you need to be aware of. It is important for the client to sign and date this form as a true record of their health and medical background.

The remainder of the form will be completed in consultation between the person responsible and yourself.

Client's medical background – With the support of the person responsible, discuss with the client the following seven questions and tick the answer 'Yes' or 'No' in the end columns as it applies to the client.	Yes ✓	No ✓
1 Has your doctor ever said that you have a heart condition and that you should only do physical activity recommended by a doctor?		
2 Do you frequently have any pains in the heart or chest?		
3 Do you often feel faint or have spells of severe dizziness?		
4 Has your doctor ever said that your blood pressure was too high?		
5 Is there any good physical reason not mentioned here why you should not undertake a programme of serious exercise?		
6 Are you over 65 years of age and not accustommed to exercise?		
Please note any other condition that would be relevant to the client undertaking physical exercise.		

To the best of my knowledge I do/do not suffer from any of the above-mentioned conditions

Client's signature _____ Date _____

The consultation between the client, the person responsible and yourself will look at the client's current fitness background, their aims and objectives, long- and short-term plans and any health and safety issues that need to be addressed.

The client's fitness background

In this section, the client will give you information on how much exercise they do in a week. This could range from virtually nothing or a couple of hours' walk a week to a 5-mile run a day.

Their aims and objectives

This section allows the client to tell you why they want to take part in physical training. Their reasons will vary from building up their strength after an injury, to just wanting to get fit or fitter, to having a specific target such as wanting to run a 10k race next year.

Two action points – long- and short-term plans

In order to identify what the client's long- and short-term plans are, you will need to look back at their aims and objectives. If we take the example of the person who wants to take part in a 10k race one year from now, then their long-term plan will be to be fit enough to take part and complete this race. Therefore the client's short-term plan may be to achieve 5k within six months.

Any health and safety factors

Again, this is linked to what the client wants to do. If they want to carry out some of their training outside (i.e. road running), then the appropriate health and safety factors here would be: weather, daylight, traffic, clothing, and so on. Also consider the client's health and whether they are on any medication. For example, if the client has asthma it will be very important that they take their inhaler with them!

Top Tip
Each centre will have its own PARQ – familiarise yourself with that centre's form.

Top Tip
You will be working alongside the person responsible when conducting a PARQ consultation with a client but try to involve yourself where you can.

Quick Test

1. What does PARQ mean?

2. What section of the PARQ will the client complete themselves?

3. What are the two plans the client has to base their objectives on?

4. What is used to formalise the client's induction to the fitness facility?

Answers 1. Physical Activity Record Questionnaire. **2.** Information about their health and medical background. **3.** long- and short-term goals. **4.** The PARQ.

Establishing a fitness baseline

What is a fitness baseline?

Before a client takes part in any fitness training, you will need to check what their baseline fitness is.

With assistance from the **person responsible**, you will assist the client in carrying out a series of different exercises that cover the components of fitness, for example: strength, muscular endurance, flexibility and cardio-respiratory. Again, the components of fitness that the client will be carrying out will need to be recorded on your assessment paperwork.

In the consultation stage (when the PARQ was completed), the client will have agreed with the person responsible on what exercises they will be doing, as this will be tailored to the client's ability and their needs. As there are a range of activities that the client may carry out, these exercises/activities may be different from the examples below.

Examples of the exercises the client could be taking part in are:

Strength: For this kind of training, you may need to ensure that there is equipment available, i.e. weights.

| Static strength training | Exercising using a range of fixed weights | High weights, low repetition, long rest in between each set of repetitions |

Muscular endurance: This can be tested in most environments. However, if you wish to use equipment (mats, weights, and so on) then this will have to be sourced before the session begins.

| Circuit training | Series of different exercises that target different parts of the body | Approx 8 stations, exercise for 45 seconds at each, resting 30 seconds in between each exercise |

Flexibility: Most flexibility exercises can be done in any environment; however, you may need something to measure the results.

| Static stretching | Stretching and holding the body to the full range of movement | Stretching body, holding body in the position for 30 seconds and then progressing |

Cardio-respiratory: This component can be tested in most environments.

| Continuous | Working at the same pace over a period of time | 10-minute cycle at 60rpm |

Recording the results of a fitness baseline test

During the PARQ consultation with the client, you will have identified which two components of fitness the client will need to be tested against while they complete their fitness baseline test.

With the person responsible, you will need to prepare for the client's baseline test by ensuring that:

- The time when you conduct the fitness baseline test is convenient to the client and you.
- The venue is appropriate – choose a venue where you can carry out all the baseline fitness tests in one place. Also, think about where you will have to do the baseline fitness retest. If the initial test is outside, will you be able to hold the retest outside as well, especially if the weather conditions change?
- Ensure that equipment is resourced – check to see if specialist testing equipment is available, accessible and is set up in plenty of time.

Once the client has completed their baseline fitness test, it is vital that you record their results afterwards, as this information will be used when you design their physical training plan. The information you will be recording, with the person responsible, will be:

- the date of the test
- the component of fitness that was tested
- the name of the kind of test that was carried out
- the result of the test.

Date	Component of fitness	Name of test	Results
1/5/07	Flexibility	Sit and reach	+1
1/5/07	Cardio-respiratory	Leger test (bleep)	4.0

Why do we record the baseline fitness results?

We record the results to enable us to:

- find out what the client's current fitness level is
- find out what components of fitness they are strong or weak in
- compare their results with others who are their age and gender
- establish how to proceed with their physical training plan.

Top Tip
You will be working with the person responsible when conducting any fitness baseline tests on clients.

Top Tip
Before you carry out fitness baseline tests, ensure you have the necessary venue and equipment in place.

Quick Test

1. What will a fitness baseline test consist of?
2. What will you need to consider when testing for muscular endurance?
3. What three preparations will you need before you carry out the fitness baseline test?
4. What will the fitness baseline test be used for?

Planning and designing a physical training plan

What to include, and for how long?

With the **person responsible**, you will be planning and designing a physical training plan for a client that lasts for a minimum of six weeks. The six-week minimum timescale is to allow the client to see any improvement they have made. Anything less will not allow the client to notice any progress in their performance.

When you design the physical training plan, you will also have to factor in rest and recovery periods for the client to avoid over-training. You will need to ensure that any period of activity is balanced with a period of inactivity (rest and recovery). For example, if the client is working on their speed component, then the short bursts of high-intensity training (hard workout) will have to be balanced against longer rest periods in order for them to recover.

Completing the physical training plan

So, by now the client will have taken part in their baseline fitness test, and you will have recorded their results. The next step is to analyse these results to ensure that the physical training plan meets the client's overall objectives.

These objectives will have been discussed before (when the client had completed their PARQ and on their baseline fitness test sheet) when the long-term and short-term goals sections had been completed. This information will help you design the physical training plan.

Short-term goals	Be able to run 5k in six months
Long-term goals	To run a 10k race next year

The goals the client has set in their PARQ will need to be transferred into their physical training plan, as this will remind you and the person responsible what their goals were if you were unable to access the client's PARQ at any time.

The client's physical training plan will have sections for you to complete on:

- the two components of fitness on which the client will be training over the agreed period of time.

You will be able to insert this information from the fitness baseline test you carried out on the client previously. The two components that you have identified will relate directly to the client's overall goals.

Detail of the two components of fitness:

1. Flexibility

2. Cardio-respiratory

- training session dates and a space to write what activities the client will be working on during each training session. This information may change each time the client is training, and should show a progression over the training period.

Training session No. 1	Training dates from: 01/07/07	to: 05/07/07
Carry out 20-minute, flexibility session		

- comments about how the client has been able to complete their physical training. These comments will also create a history of each training session, with notes of how the client has performed (well or badly) and any modifications that were made, or should be made in the future. There is also a section for you and your assessor to sign and date at the end of each physical training session.

Comments:

The client's hamstring flexibility is still poor. Will include some partner stretches in next week's programmes.

Be SMART!

When you are planning and organising the physical training plan, it is important that any goals that you set are 'SMART'

Specific   Stating the outcome you want clearly

Measurable   How you will know when it has been achieved

Attainable   Ensuring it is possible to achieve your goals

Realistic   Ensuring you have realistic goals

Time phased Set a deadline for achieving your goals

Top Tip
Ensure that the components of fitness are suitable to the overall aims and objectives of the client and their needs.

Top Tip
Ensure that all sections on the physical training plan are completed, signed and dated.

Quick Test

1. How long will the physical training plan last for?

2. When planning a physical training plan, what factors will you have to build in?

3. What information will need to be transferred on to the physical training plan from the PARQ?

4. What does the T stand for in SMART?

Answers 1. Minimum of six weeks. **2.** Periods of activity and inactivity. **3.** Short- and long-term goals, and the two components of fitness. **4.** Time-phased.

Assessing physical training plans

Client reviews

At all times during the review process with the client, you will be working with the **person responsible** to assist the client to carry out a review of their progress since the last time you met with them. Reviews should be:

- regular – for example, once a week. This will ensure that you can monitor the physical training plan regularly and that the client is following the plan. It will also ensure that the client's training plan is updated regularly, which will keep up the client's motivation. A client will usually have a review of their fitness programme at least once a week; however, it is important that no more than two weeks go by without a review of their performance and progression.

- held at an agreed time and place – it is easier to confirm a time and place at the end of the previous review, as this will ensure that you and the client are able to meet. However, be flexible and be prepared for times and places to change – for example, because of weather conditions or if you are unable to access the usual facilities.

The client should bring to their review their physical training plan and any other training diary/logs they may have.

By reviewing with the client, you can ask them how they think the programme is progressing. They will be able to give you information on:

- whether the programme is too easy – this will mean that, for example, the duration that the client is running for may need to be increased

- identifying aspects of the training that are too difficult, therefore the type of exercise may need to be decreased

- if the client missed any training sessions and finding out the reasons why

- any issues relating to injury – has the client sustained an injury since the last review? This would mean that the fitness programme would need to be modified as a result.

Monitoring and modifying physical training plans

Monitoring is where you watch and check a situation carefully over a set period of time. By doing this, you will discover the outcomes of the task that the client was set.

With the person responsible, you will be monitoring the client while they carry out their physical training according to the plan that the client, the person responsible and you devised. Through monitoring, you can observe the client as they work through their physical training plan and can make small changes along the way to enable the client to 'keep on track'. You will be able to gather information about how well they are progressing and achieving their goals that were set out in the beginning.

You may need to modify the client's training plan for a number of reasons:

- the client is finding it difficult to achieve the goals set – therefore you may need to break down the training into smaller, more achievable stages
- the client has achieved aspects of their goals sooner than what was planned for – as a result of this, you will need to set more difficult targets to keep the client interested and motivated, and they will then have new goals to meet
- training venues unavailable – this could be due to the weather or the facility being closed on a public holiday.

All monitoring and modifications will also need to take into account feedback and comments from the clients on how well they have performed since their review. This could affect the type of future training – for example, if the client has sustained an injury or is unable to attend their next training session. All modifications will need to be noted down on their training plan for future reference and for the client's next review.

Top Tip

Find out from the person responsible how often you will be reviewing the client's physical training plan, with the client.

Top Tip

You will be assisting the person responsible when you monitor and modify any aspect of the client's physical training plan

Quick Test

1. What should the client bring with them to the review?

2. Why would you need to know if the client has sustained an injury?

3. What is monitoring?

4. Give three examples why you may need to modify the client's training plan.

Reassessing the components of fitness

Why the same conditions?

From the beginning, we have subjected a client to a range of fitness tests and recorded these results. The reason why we have to carry out any retesting of these fitness components is to ensure the reliability and validity of the tests.

If you recreate the exact conditions as in the initial baseline fitness test, this will then mean that your test is valid. To do this, you must ensure that:

- If the test was carried out inside, then the retest must be carried out in the same place. To have the retest outside would mean that, for example, weather conditions could affect the client's performance, therefore the test would be invalid.

- If the test was done on grass, then you would have to ensure that the client has access to the same conditions to carry out their retesting. Again, this will affect their results if they had, for example, carried out their baseline fitness test on a tarmac surface.

- If equipment was used (for example, the client cycled for 20 minutes to test their cardio-respiratory component of fitness), then exactly the same type of equipment must be used, and the test must be performed under the same conditions – i.e. the client will be cycling for 20 minutes, not running!

Retesting is not the final part of the client's physical training: it can be used as part of a larger progression, and it will measure improvement as the client's goals continue to be reviewed and evaluated.

On your assessment papers, there are tables for you to complete to record the client's reassessment of the components of fitness you tested in the beginning.

Review of client's physical training plan

A review should take place once the client's physical training has been completed, and the review should involve the client. During your assessment you will be assisting the preson responsible with this review and complete the relevant assessment paperwork in full.

When you are reviewing with the client:

1. you will be asking them general questions that relate overall to the physical training and the programme design

2. you need to note down two aspects of the client's fitness programming activity that went well (strengths) and aspects that needed to be changed (weaknesses).

Examples of the positive aspects:

- That relate to the client's own personal fitness
- The environment in which the physical training was delivered
- **Health and safety** measures that were put in place to help the client carry out their physical training plan.

Examples of the negative aspects:

- The client's own personal issues (motivation to achieve goals; illness, and so on)
- Unable to access facilities to allow the client to carry out their physical training
- Modifications to training plan were inappropriate (e.g. increasing the difficulty beyond the client's capability).

The review process will also allow the client to give feedback on your strengths and weaknesses in relation to developing the fitness programme. The client will have the opportunity to note down three aspects of:

- Your strengths – appropriate modifications to the physical plan, your ability to recognise the necessary health and safety factors, and so on.
- Your weaknesses – more awareness of the components of fitness and to identify which two the client had to work on to achieve their goal, and so on.

At the end of this review with the client, you will be able to identify two action points for the client to focus on when they continue their physical training, and two action points for you to reflect on and to be aware of the next time you assist a client with their fitness programming.

Top Tip
It is best to plan ahead where you will conduct the baseline fitness test, as the retest will have to be done under the same conditions to ensure an accurate result.

Top Tip
You will be assisting the person responsible when you carry out the baseline fitness retest and the client reviews.

Quick Test

1. When we retest the client's fitness baseline, what must we ensure?

2. What may the fitness baseline retest be used for?

3. When should the review take place?

4. What two aspects will the client be giving feedback on?

Answers: 1. The validity and reliability of the test. **2.** Client progression and further goals. **3.** Once the physical training has been completed. **4.** Positive and negative aspects of the fitness programme.

Assisting with activity sessions – scope

Gathering information

This Unit is designed to enable you to assist the person responsible when planning and delivering activity sessions for groups and individuals. You will learn how to gather information about:

- The type of activity
- The equipment to be used – this will include safety, participants' and your own equipment
- Where the activity will take place
- Relevant health and safety issues – this will also include issues relating to predictable changes of circumstances
- Risk assessment for the activity
- Emergency procedures – medical and another type of emergency.

For your assessment, you will meet with the person responsible and agree what component of the activity you will be assisting with. You will then have to demonstrate that you can collect relevant information about the activity, venue, equipment and its participants and complete a risk assessment. This information will then be used to help you plan your component of the activity.

As you will be taking part in assisting with the component within activity sessions, you have to ensure that you arrive on time, in the correct location and dressed appropriately for the sessions. You will also have to assist the person responsible to ensure that the clients have the correct clothing, equipment and activity information at the beginning of the activity sessions.

During the activity session you will be expected to assist the person responsible to give instructions, explanations and demonstrations to participants and respond to questions from participants, observe participants and give them feedback. If you encounter any problems, it is important that you refer them to the person responsible for the activity.

At the end of the activity session, you will be helping to store the activity equipment and then assist with reviewing of the activity with the participants. After the session has ended, you will meet and review your performance with the person responsible.

Organisational procedures

During the activity, you will be expected to follow the centre/organisation's procedures and show that you can demonstrate what your role would be in the event of an emergency. You will have to complete this part of the Unit in a 'realistic working environment' and take part in a range of different emergency situations; one will be a medical emergency (i.e. a minor or major illness or injury), and another will be a different type of emergency, for example:

+ Fire
+ Suspicious strangers
+ Missing people
+ Theft

It will be important that, if you encounter any problems, you inform the person responsible. When you have attended to the emergency, you will have to ensure that you complete any reports relevant to that emergency. At the end of the emergency situation, you will review your performance with the person responsible.

At the end of your assessment, you will develop a personal action plan which will be in relation to the activity sessions. This action plan will be conducted with the person responsible, where you will gather relevant information about how well you performed during the activity session and when you carried out emergency procedures. With this information, the review will focus on your strengths and weaknesses in relation to the activity session, and this will form the basis of your personal action plan for future activity sessions.

Employability skills in this Unit

In this Unit, you will have the opportunity to develop a range of **employability skills**. These are:

2. Review and self-evaluation
4. Setting targets for self and others
5. Positive attitude to learning
6. Planning and preparation
7. Customer care/dealing with clients
8. Time keeping
9. Taking advice from others
10. Wearing appropriate dress
11. Giving advice and feedback to others
12. Awareness of health and safety issues

Top Tip
Look out for the symbol to see where the **employability skills** have been covered.

Top Tip
Remember, any words in GREEN are explained in the GLOSSARY section on pages 94–95.

Candidates' roles and responsibilities

Information needed for the activity plan

All coaches, instructors, tutors, and so, on have had to gather information about the activity or course they will be taking. In this Unit, you will be assisting with a component of an activity session and therefore having to gather relevant information together in order to plan and prepare for it.

It is important that you gather information relevant to the activity, as this will give you an insight into all the little things that you need to consider before meeting any participants for an activity – for example, what equipment you will need.

With the person responsible, you will agree what your role will be during the activity session and what component of the activity session you will be assisting with. This will then help you with the activity session plan.

Before you go and write up an activity session plan, you will need to have collected the relevant information about the activity. For your assessment, you will have to demonstrate that you can plan an activity for an individual and another activity for a group. The different types of information you need to collect for this plan will be:

- The time and date of when the activity session will take place, and how long it will last
- What the aims are for the activity
- Where the activity will take place
- The number of participants in the group
- The part of the activity session you will be planning for
- The kind of equipment you will need
- Plan for any changes to the original plan
- Plan for emergencies and incidents

Once you have collected the information together and written up your activity session plan, you will need to get it approved by the person responsible.

Equipment for the activity

In consultation with the person responsible, you will need to find out whether the equipment you have planned to use is available for your activity session. This is because, in most sport and recreation centres/facilities, there will be more than one group using the centre and its facilities.

Another factor to consider is whether equipment needs to be assembled before a session starts, as this will affect the activity session timings. This will depend on the type of activity and on where it is taking place.

The types of equipment are split up into four main categories:

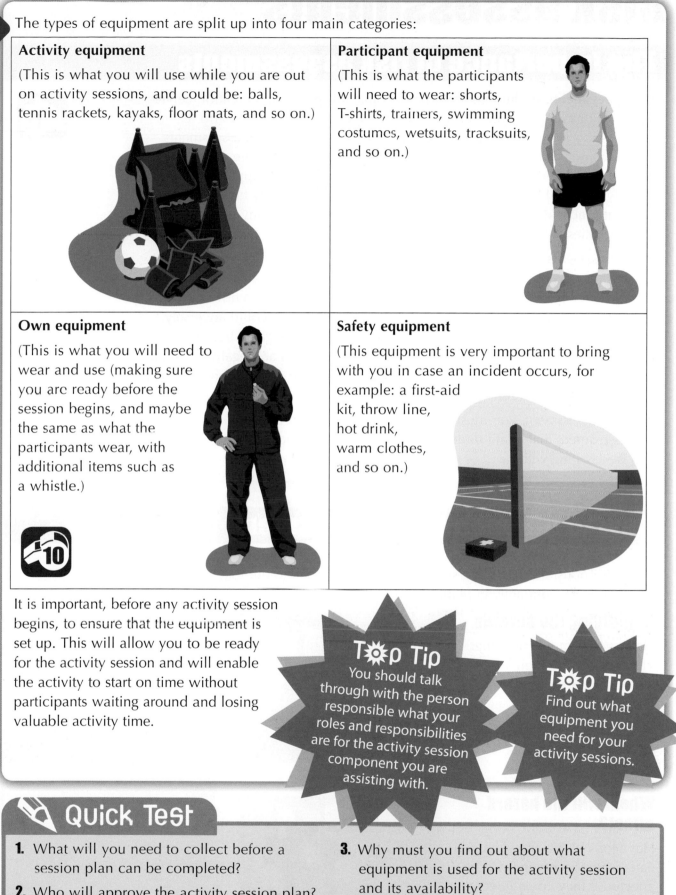

Activity equipment

(This is what you will use while you are out on activity sessions, and could be: balls, tennis rackets, kayaks, floor mats, and so on.)

Participant equipment

(This is what the participants will need to wear: shorts, T-shirts, trainers, swimming costumes, wetsuits, tracksuits, and so on.)

Own equipment

(This is what you will need to wear and use (making sure you are ready before the session begins, and maybe the same as what the participants wear, with additional items such as a whistle.)

Safety equipment

(This equipment is very important to bring with you in case an incident occurs, for example: a first-aid kit, throw line, hot drink, warm clothes, and so on.)

It is important, before any activity session begins, to ensure that the equipment is set up. This will allow you to be ready for the activity session and will enable the activity to start on time without participants waiting around and losing valuable activity time.

Top Tip
You should talk through with the person responsible what your roles and responsibilities are for the activity session component you are assisting with.

Top Tip
Find out what equipment you need for your activity sessions.

Quick Test

1. What will you need to collect before a session plan can be completed?

2. Who will approve the activity session plan?

3. Why must you find out about what equipment is used for the activity session and its availability?

4. What are the four categories of equipment?

Risk assessments

The importance of risk assessments

Risk assessments are an important process that all sport and recreation centres/organisations have to undertake by examining what could cause harm to anyone who uses a centre and its facilities. By carrying out risk assessments, you measure whether you have taken enough precautions for the activity or whether you need to do more to prevent further harm from happening. They identify potential hazards and how these can be made safe by highlighting the relevant practical steps to reduce the risk for the centre and any groups using their facilities.

Risk assessments cover not only activities but also potential hazards in the centre/organisation – for example, changing areas, kitchens/cafés, car parking facilities etc. In centres and organisations, risk assessments are carried out to prevent accidents and ill health for their staff and clients. It could adversely affect their business if a client or a member of staff takes legal action against the company, and they end up in court. Therefore centres are legally required to assess any risks posed to staff and clients who use the facilities and to put in control measures to reduce these risks.

For your assessment, you must demonstrate that you can complete aspects of a risk assessment that relate directly to the component of activity sessions that you will be assisting with.

How to fill out a risk assessment

When you complete a risk assessment, you will get help and advice from the person responsible. The basic steps below will help you to put together your risk assessment for your activity plan.

Identifying the hazards

Have a look at this drawing. The hazard in this picture is the **water on the floor**.

Whom will the hazard affect?

Have look at this drawing. You can see that **everyone** will be affected if they come in contact with the water on the floor.

How will the hazard affect everyone?

The hazard effect here has been that the individual has **slipped** in the water and fallen on to the floor.

Putting in control measures

Now you can see that the control measures here have been put in place by putting up a 'Slippery floor' **sign** to inform everyone that there is a hazard ahead. Now, when anyone approaches the water on the floor, they will know that it is there and will walk round it safely.

Ratings

Ratings are given to show the seriousness of a hazard. These ratings are on a scale of **1 (Low)**, **2 (Medium)**, **3 (High)**:

	Risk rating
1 What would be the risk rating for someone who has slipped and fallen?	2
2 What would be the likelihood of it actually happening?	2
Multiplying these two figures together will give you a risk rating before you put in those control measures (the 'slippery floor' sign)	= 4
3 What would happen to this rating when you DO put the control measures in place? It will reduce it to:	1
What would the **NEW risk rating** for the wet floor be, now you have the 'slippery floor' sign in place? (To find this out, you need to multiply points number 2 and 3.) As you can see, the risk has been significantly reduced by identifying the hazard and putting up a sign.	= 2

Top Tip
When writing up a risk assessment, only note down hazards that will affect the activity you are assisting with!

Top Tip
Risk ratings are a way of seeing how serious a hazard is. When you have put in your control measures, this rating will fall, therefore significantly reducing the risk to everyone.

Quick Test

1. What is the important process of identifying potential hazards?

2. Who can be affected by a hazard?

3. What was the control measure put in place to warn people of the hazard?

4. What is the risk rating scale?

Answers: 1. Risk assessments. **2.** Everyone. **3.** A sign. **4.** 1 (Low), 2 (Medium), 3 (High).

Planning for an individual or a group of clients

Activity session plans

Every coach, tutor, instructor etc. who has taken an activity session at some point has completed a session plan for a group or for an individual. An activity session plan is a written guide in order to achieve the aims and objectives of the session.

It will provide specific information about equipment, participants and an outline of the component of the session you will be assisting with. Plans are made to give the session some structure (showing a breakdown of what is contained in the activity session, including timings) and will allow you to cover all the main aims and objectives of the activity in the allotted time.

When you assist the person responsible with an activity session plan, it will be based on an a component of the activity that you will have agreed before with the person responsible. It is essential that all activity session plans are completed **BEFORE** the activity begins, as this will allow you and the person responsible:

- to decide whether all content is correct – the person responsible will check through, and, if there is nothing to change, you can then go and assist on the activity session

   or

- to decide whether content of the activity plan needs alteration – this could be additional material that needs inserted, deletions where some of the content is not required or is inappropriate, or some modifications where most of the content is applicable but needs some changes made

   and

- a final check to ensure that the plan is complete before the activity goes ahead.

Once the plan has been approved, the **person responsible** will then sign and date to indicate that the activity session plan is now ready for you to assist with the component.

Activity session plans: structure and contents

For your **assessment**, you will be asked to complete an activity session plan. The assessment plan will already be drawn up with the necessary headings informing you what to write in the spaces next to them. The assessor will issue you with these forms and any other assessment paperwork you may need to assist you with the completion of the activity session plan – for example, the risk assessment form. In some cases, you could be using a different type of session plan, so it is always best to check that they have the same content as the ones supplied by the awarding body.

Activity session plans should contain the following:

What the activity is and where it is taking place	Activity: Nature walk Venue: Forest track, Loch Lomond
Day, time, and how long it will last for – e.g. 3 hours	Date: 14/07/07 Time: From: 9.30am To: 12.30 pm
Information about the group or individual – e.g. health issues	Info on group: 2 participants have Asthma
What equipment you will be using – e.g. equipment for you, for the activity, for safety and for the participants	Own equip: rucksack, boots, waterproofs Activity equip: group shelter, radio Safety equip: first-aid kit Participant equip: boots, waterproofs
If equipment needs to be set up before the session begins – note down the equipment, for example, goals for football	Equip that needs to be set up: Ensure that relevant safety equipment and group shelters are available for the day
Noting down any predictable changes of circumstances – e.g. weather	Predictable changes of circumstances: Weather conditions changing and participant emergencies
Main aim of the session – e.g. individual skills, teamwork, and so on	Aim of session: give participants an experience in nature by using their senses
Your involvement in the activity – e.g. your role during the activity	My involvement: to assist the person responsible with two activities
What are the main teaching points – e.g. how to use a kayak paddle when kayaking forward	Teaching points: assist participants with an activity. 1) that used their smelling sense 2) that used their listening sense

Top Tip
The person responsible will be able to help you with supplying the relevant information necessary to complete all sections of the activity session plan.

Top Tip
The person responsible for taking the activity session will sign off your activity session plan, and can be a coach, instructor, tutor or teacher.

Quick Test

1. When should activity session plans be completed?

2. Who will sign and date the activity session plan once it has been approved?

3. When will you need to complete your activity session plans for?

4. Give an example of the kind of information you will need to complete in the section for information on the group.

Answers: 1. Before. **2.** The person responsible. **3.** For your assessment. **4.** Health issues.

Delivering the component

Instructions, explanations and demonstrations

It is important that, when you are delivering a component of an activity session, you are ready to go! What this means is that you need to be mentally and physically prepared for the activity session by:

- Knowing the sporting activity that you will be taking part in, as you will otherwise not be able to perform any explanations or demonstrations adequately

- Knowing what component you are going to be assisting with

- Being appropriately dressed before the session begins, being on time and having the correct equipment ready to use

- Setting up equipment before you meet the clients/participants.

Delivering the component is done in three ways. These are:

- Instructions – this is where you may give participants simple, uncomplicated tasks to do (for example, run round the track three times)

- Explanations – sometimes you will need to go into a bit more detail about a particular instruction or demonstration (for example, in kayaking, when you forward paddle, ensure that the whole paddle blade is in the water)

- Demonstrations – this is when you physically show the participants what you want them to do and how to do something (for example, showing participants how to nock an arrow on a string in archery).

During your instructions, explanations and demonstrations, it is important to allow the participants to ask questions. Remember, even though you know the activity and exercises within a sporting activity, you have to understand that participants might not, and you must be patient and be prepared to go over things again.

Out of all the delivery techniques, when you demonstrate to participants, they will always understand what you want them to do. As they say: a picture speaks a thousand words.

Explaining the activity

How you explain the activity or tasks to a group will mean the difference between the participants carrying out the tasks you set them, or not. Consider the following when explaining an activity or task to the group:

- Talk slowly and clearly – your participants will understand you better if you do this. Also consider the environment: are you in a big hall, or outside in windy conditions? You may need to change the way you talk to suit where the activity is taking place.
- Face in the direction of the group – consider again the environment you are in. By facing the group, your voice will project towards them and they should hear you better than if you are facing away. Also, you may need to think about the different types of participants in your group – could they be hard of hearing and require you to look at them so they can lip read?
- Be prepared to repeat your explanation – it may be beneficial to repeat yourself a few times. This way, the group will take in all the information you are giving them, especially if the sporting activity is new and you have asked them to do more than one task.

Demonstrations can show participants clearly what you want them to do. Not all participants may understand what you are saying, especially if they are new to the sport. Consider the following when carrying out demonstrations to the group:

- Where are the group positioned – behind you, in front, in a circle
- Position yourself so that you can see all the participants – if you can see them, they can see you.
- If demonstrating outside, consider the weather conditions. Where would it be best to demonstrate: sheltered area, away from the sun etc.
- Slow your demonstrations down
- Repeat your demonstrations

Top Tip
Have you tried explaining an activity without talking?

Top Tip
Practise the sport or activity whenever you can. The more experienced you are, the more confident you will become when you have to instruct, explain and demonstrate for a group or an individual.

Top Tip
When you are assisting with the component of an activity session, choose an appropriate environment (e.g. with your back to the sun or the group's backs to a window or door).

Quick Test

1. What will you need to be before you assist with the component of an activity session?

2. What are the three components that deal with delivering an activity session to participants?

3. What will you need to do so that the group can understand your instructions and explanations?

4. Why is positioning yourself important when you are demonstrating to a group?

Storage of equipment

Managing time

Not every centre will have someone assigned specifically to setting up, taking down and storing of equipment. Therefore you will need to leave enough time in the session to do these tasks.

When you plan for an activity session, you will always need to leave enough time at the end of the session to tidy, clean and store the equipment away either in the store or in a specified place ready for storage. It is not uncommon to involve the participants and other people in the group in this process, as it will encourage them to have ownership of the equipment, help with large or awkward equipment and get the task done more quickly.

It is important if you are involving participants to assist you with moving any type of equipment, that you take into consideration the relevant health and safety factors. These will be:

- What the ages of the participants are – you can't expect six-year-olds to carry large and heavy pieces of equipment!
- With any group, you may need to brief them before carrying out any tasks that involve the moving of equipment – this could be how to lift it safely to avoid the participants injuring themselves.
- If the equipment has to be carried over a long distance, you may need to brief the group about stopping and having a short break before continuing back to the centre.

When you go to store the equipment, you will have to ensure that it is ready for future use. This is done by ensuring that the equipment is:

- clean – this will stop some pieces of equipment from rusting or corroding, and it will ensure that the equipment is ready to use for the next activity
- stored tidily – this will ensure that the equipment is easily found for the next session
- stored safely – to prevent staff or participants from having any accidents.

Review of session with clients

Points to cover

Usually, the content of what you review with participants will be linked with their aims for the activity session, for example:

- Fun and enjoyment
- Promoting teamwork
- Environmental
- Developing individuals' skill levels

Reviews will be different for an individual and a group of participants, therefore the person responsible for the activity will lead the review, and you will assist them. The reviews will encourage participants to 'have their say' on what they thought about the activity session and how well they performed as individuals or as a group, which would all depend on what their initial aims and objectives were.

The review may be an informal or a formal session:

- Informal sessions will generally be a chat, or you may use specific review games which involve the participants to give feedback on how the session went, as well as allowing them to identify any aspects that were good or bad.
- Formal review sessions may involve the participants being issued with specific review material that could be a formal log book, questionnaires or specialist reviewing materials. This may be the case if the group of participants are schoolchildren and their activity or experience is linked with their schoolwork.

Again depending on the aims and objectives, participants may need to record their reviews. This can be done by means of a simple questionnaire or a more formal type of log book which can be used for other purposes, for example, Community Sports Leader Award or the John Muir Award.

You may wish to consider keeping copies of any reviews that take place, as this will be good material for your own review with the person responsible at the end of the activity session or for the completion of this Unit.

(Speech bubbles: "How did you enjoy the activity?" "Great!")

Top Tip
Make sure, when equipment is stored, that it is clean and serviceable – ready for the next group to use. If you need to remove the equipment from store because it is unserviceable, inform the person responsible first and follow their instructions.

Top Tip
Make the review session fun, and include all participants in a group. The person responsible will be able to give you different types of reviewing techniques.

Quick Test

1. What must you incorporate into your activity session plan that relates to equipment?
2. Why would you involve members of the group to assist with putting away activity equipment?
3. What are the two types of review processes?
4. How can formal reviews be recorded?

Answers 1. Tidy, clean and store equipment. **2.** Encourage them to have ownership. Assist with large or awkward pieces, task will get done quicker. **3.** Formal and informal. **4.** Log book, questionnaires.

Emergencies in the sport and recreation environment

Dealing with emergencies

In any sport and recreation environment, all kinds of **emergencies** may have to be dealt with, some minor and others major. In this Unit, you will have to demonstrate your ability to carry out tasks and the correct procedures when an emergency occurs, specifically in a sport and recreation setting.

If you have completed the Skills for Work – Intermediate 1 course, you will have gained a great deal of knowledge of the different types of illnesses, injuries and emergencies you may encounter. However, do not worry; if you did not complete the Intermediate 1 course; your tutor will need to cover these important aspects of the course in order to bring you up to the required level.

You will find that all these types of emergencies will be assessed in a 'real sporting environment' where you will be operating. This means that, when you are on activity sessions or when you are in a sports or leisure centre performing your duties, the emergencies will be related directly to that environment, not in a classroom! However, for training purposes you will probably be in a type of classroom, where you will learn the necessary knowledge, your roles and responsibilities and what to do in a specific emergency.

For your assessment, you will need to take part in two different emergency situations:

+ 1 × medical – this can be either an injury or an illness (major or minor)
+ 1 × other type of emergency – fire, missing person, theft, suspicious strangers etc.

It is recognised in most qualifications that require any candidates to perform tasks which are 'reactive' that there is some flexibility given in the way they are assessed. What this means is that you cannot plan when someone will fall over and break their leg, or when the centre will go on fire!

So, what happens then?

It will be at the discretion of the tutors and the centre to set up role-play scenarios in the sport or leisure centres where you will have to demonstrate how you would deal with the specific emergency which covers the necessary aspects of the Unit requirements for your assessment.

Scenarios and real emergencies

In this particular Unit, candidates are required to carry out **scenarios** to reinforce their learning when dealing with **accident** and emergency situations. Scenarios will cover most aspects of the knowledge and understanding of the Skills for Work Unit and will give candidates a chance to perform their duties in a 'safe environment'. These scenarios will always be planned.

Scenarios are simulations of real events or incidents. In scenarios, you can play a range of different roles; you could be the casualty or a member of staff coming to the aid of a casualty. These scenarios will be designed to be 'realistic' and therefore should be set in a sport and recreation environment for your assessments.

When you start your scenarios, you will be given a briefing sheet which will explain what part you are to play and what to do. As each scenario may be different, you may be working in pairs or in a small group consisting of other members of your group. Sometimes centres may use other members of staff or groups to assist you in the scenario, and they will have been briefed as to what roles they will play.

It is important to remember that you are only expected to carry out the tasks set within your level of responsibility in any emergency situation.

For example

Who does what	The Scenario
Candidate No. 1 (is the casualty)	You were running along the side of the swimming pool and slipped, banging the back of your head. You now have to pretend that your head really hurts.
Candidate No. 2 (is the rescuer)	You have been alerted by a member of the public that someone has fallen over and hurt their head. You will approach the person and ask questions, reassure the casualty and find the person responsible to deal with the accident.

T⚙p Tip
If you have had to deal with a 'real' emergency on your course, DO include the relevant reports/information in your assessment material.

T⚙p Tip
Taking part in scenarios can be fun, but remember that they are representing what a real emergency can look like. Practising scenarios regularly will prepare you for when it really happens.

Quick Test

1. Where will your assessment be held for dealing with emergencies?

2. What duties will you carry out in the event of an emergency?

3. What are simulations?

4. What are simulations designed to be?

Answers 1. In a sporting environment. **2.** To the level of my ability and level of responsibility. **3.** Simulations of real events or incidents. **4.** Realistic.

Following emergency procedures

Performing duties

In this Unit, you will have to demonstrate that you can perform a range of duties in an emergency situation. When you are carrying out these duties, you will be under the supervision of the person responsible and it is very important that you perform your duties to your level of responsibility, to the skill level to which you have been trained (i.e. first-aid course). You must follow the instructions given from the person responsible and must comply with centre or organisational procedures at all times.

These emergency procedures will be split up into:

+ Medical – dealing with illnesses and injuries (major or minor)

    and

+ Other emergencies – missing people, suspicious strangers, fire, theft etc.

What do you do in an emergency?

When you do encounter someone who has sustained an injury or has an illness, or you experience another type of emergency, there are a few points that you must pay particular attention to:

+ **Scene safety** is above all the most important aspect of any emergency. You must make sure that it is safe to enter a room/building or go near a casualty; this will ensure that you will not become a casualty yourself by falling debris, smoke inhalation, and so on. You must also think about whether it is safe to attend to any injured person or to someone who has an illness.

+ Ensure that you have informed the person responsible – give them relevant information, for example, where the emergency is, how many people are involved, when it happened etc.

+ Follow their instructions – these will usually involve you carrying out tasks relating to the specific emergency, for example, getting first-aid kits, doing roll-calls at the fire-assembly point etc.

+ Be able to deal with problems that may arise – be able to solve basic problems and report these back to the person responsible, for example, finding an alternative way of calling the emergency services if the phone is out of order.

+ Ensure that any information relating to the casualty or emergency is kept **confidential**.

Safety first!

In any accident or emergency situation, **health and safety** is very important. You have to ensure the safety of yourself above anyone else, no matter how bad the situation. For example:

+ When you see a casualty who has injured themselves, you have to think about what has caused the injury in the first place, ensuring you will not do the same thing as the casualty and therefore become one yourself!

+ When you see an emergency incident, i.e. a fire, the first thing you must think about is your safety – getting yourself out of the building or away from the fire, assisting the person responsible and following their instructions. What about a missing person? Your first step would be to tell the person responsible about what has happened and follow their instructions. Their instructions may be to go and find that person – think about the sport and recreation environment you are in and whether it could be potentially dangerous to you to go off and look for the person.

Think first!

Before you go rushing into a situation, think about the following points first:

+ Find out about the incident and inform the person responsible: the more information you have the better. You can then pass on this information to the person responsible, who will then make a decision on what action to take.

+ Assess the scene: look around you and see whether it is safe to continue.

+ Report back only to the person responsible. In any situation, it is important that you report back to the correct person. Where a major incident has taken place, for example, major emergency (fire), organisations will have procedures which all staff must follow, for example, not talking to the press or publicising casualty information.

+ Wearing correct **Personal Protective Equipment (PPE)**: all staff must wear PPE to ensure that they do not harm themselves while carrying out duties in emergencies, for example, first-aid gloves.

Top Tip
When you are in any emergency situation, it is important that you know what your roles and responsibilities are. If you are unsure, talk to the person responsible.

Top Tip
Always assess the scene of an emergency. This will always avoid you getting hurt and becoming a casualty yourself. If it doesn't look safe, don't go in!

Quick Test

1. What must you do in an emergency situation?

2. What is the most important action you will take in an emergency situation?

3. To whom will you report any information relating to an emergency situation?

4. What PPE may you have to wear in a first-aid emergency?

Answers 1. Follow the instructions given by the person responsible. **2.** Assess the scene. **3.** The person responsible. **4.** Disposable gloves.

Types of emergencies

What are injuries?

A **minor injury** is where treatment can be administered by a first-aider (the person responsible). All organisations will have first-aiders on site who are qualified to the appropriate level required by the organisation. For example, an outdoor instructor will be trained in how to deal with casualties specifically in the outdoors, and a pool lifeguard with situations relating to water. These can be the only person or people dealing with first aid in the centre or organisation; or first-aiding may be part of their work duty.

It is important to note that in some cases a minor injury may need medical assistance to confirm that the casualty has no other injuries. For example, what looks to be a sprained ankle in a child could also mean they have a broken bone in their ankle!

A **major injury** is where treatment must be administered by medical assistance, for example, paramedics, doctors etc. Although first-aiders will be the people who will be with the casualty first to assess their injuries, they cannot give any medication for pain relief or set broken bones, for example, so the casualty WILL need to receive medical assistance in a hospital.

Major injuries are different from minor injuries. This is because these types of injuries can be potentially life threatening and immediate action will need to be taken to prevent the injury from worsening.

Top Tip

Never forget: although something can begin as a minor incident, it can quickly become a major incident if not dealt with appropriately. If unsure of the severity of the injury or illness, consult the person responsible and follow their instructions.

What are illnesses?

A minor illness is where the casualty usually has a history of the illness, although not in all cases. **The first-aider (the person responsible) should be able to deal with any minor illness** and if necessary seek medical assistance.

A major illness is where the casualty has a past history (not in all cases) of the illness and needs immediate **medical assistance**. The role of the person responsible (who will be the first-aider) will be to make the casualty as comfortable as possible and carry out treatment to their illness until medical assistance arrives.

What to do in other types of emergencies

Fire
+ get out of the building/centre or away from the fire
+ assemble at the fire-assembly point
+ assist the person responsible and follow their instructions
+ **DO NOT** re-enter the building or go near a fire

Unlawful entry and theft

+ leave everything the way it was found, and do not touch anything
+ inform the person responsible as soon as possible
+ make a note of your actions, including times and dates
+ note details down of the incident as you had found it, and give this to the person responsible
+ do not allow anyone else to enter the area until you are told to
+ follow all instructions given by the person responsible at all times

Theft

When an **incident of theft** has taken place of someone's belongings, it is also important to do the following:

+ make a note of what the person is saying, and include dates, times and the person's name and address
+ give reassurance to the person
+ inform the person responsible as soon as possible
+ pass on the information you have collected
+ follow all instructions given by the person responsible at all times

Missing people

+ inform the person responsible
+ have a good look around the organisation/centre
+ gather information from people
+ carry out any instructions given to you by the person responsible

Suspicious strangers

+ inform the person responsible and explain your suspicions
+ follow the instructions given by the person responsible

If you are approached by someone else who is **reporting a suspicious stranger**, it is important that you:

+ note any details down that are given to you
+ give the details to the person responsible as soon as possible
+ follow the instructions given by the person responsible

Top Tip
Whenever you are faced with an emergency situation, never deal with it yourself; leave the scene untouched and always inform the person responsible.

Quick Test

1. What is a minor injury?
2. What is a major illness?
3. What must you not do when you have exited a building that is on fire?
4. What must you do if someone reports a suspicious stranger?

Answers 1. When treatment can be administered by a first-aider. **2.** When treatment requires immediate medical assistance. **3.** Re-enter. **4.** Inform the person responsible.

Emergency health and safety

Reporting and recording of emergencies

In all centres and organisations, it is a legal requirement that any accidents and emergencies are recorded in some way.

+ The first stage of any **report** will be a verbal report to a senior colleague or line manager. In your case, it will be the person responsible.

+ The second stage will be to complete a record of events that led to the injury, illness or other type of emergency. For this purpose, the centre will have specific forms for an injury/illness and, for example, a fire. Your role will be to assist the person responsible in the completion of these forms.

+ The third stage of reporting will be the forms which need to be completed in the event of a major emergency (e.g. a broken leg). In this case, you will not be asked to contribute to the completion of this form. It is usually the manager who will gather information together about the incident and complete the Health and Safety Executive (RIDDOR) form.

Top Tip
Make sure you know how to complete accident and emergency report forms.

An example of an Accident Report Form

This form is to report incidences of: near miss, injury, physical violence, verbal abuse, dangerous occurrences and notifiable diseases.

An example of an Emergency Report Form

This form is to report incidences of: fire, security or other types of emergencies.

IMPORTANT!

No matter how small an incident, it must be reported. Whether it be an accident or an emergency, these **report** forms are used to keep a record of the history of incidents and to see if there is an accident trend. This information can be called upon as evidence in court.

It is important that all reports are stored in a safe location and comply with the **Data Protection Act**.

RIDDOR

RIDDOR means: **"Reporting of Injuries, Diseases and Dangerous Occurrences Regulations"**.

All companies (centres and organisations) have to adhere to these 1995 Regulations. It places a legal duty on all employers, anyone who is self-employed or anyone who has people in control of premises, to report on any major injuries, diseases, dangerous occurrences (including near misses) or deaths that have occurred on or in their centre or organisation.

RIDDOR covers:

- deaths
- major injuries
- over-three-day injuries – where an employee or self-employed person is away from work or unable to perform their normal work duties for more than three consecutive days
- injuries to members of the public or people not at work where they are taken from the scene of an accident to hospital
- some work-related diseases
- dangerous occurrences – where something happens that does not result in an injury, but could have done
- CORGI-registered gas fitters must also report dangerous gas fittings they find, and gas conveyors/suppliers must report certain flammable gas incidents.

It is a legal requirement for these centres or organisations to report any major injuries, diseases or dangerous occurrences as soon as possible, which will enable the Health and Safety Executive and local authorities to look at these incidents and assess whether they require investigating further. Most major and serious incidents will always be investigated. These types of incidents are rare, but may happen.

In most centres or organisations, the person who completes any major report, such as a RIDDOR, will usually be a senior member of staff, which could be the person responsible. It is your duty to ensure that you contribute to the details, giving your account of the incident.

Top Tip

It is the responsibility of all staff in a facility to report any injuries that occur to participants, clients or other members of staff.

✎ Quick Test

1. How many stages are there in the reporting of accidents and emergencies?

2. Why are accident and emergency reports completed?

3. What does RIDDOR stand for?

4. Do centres have an obligation to report any incidents to RIDDOR?

Answers 1. Three. 2. To keep a history of the incident and to see if there is an accident trend. 3. Reporting of Injuries, Diseases and Dangerous Occurrences Regulations. 4. Yes.

Developing a personal action plan

What to include

For your assessment, you will be expected to complete the relevant paperwork with the person responsible about your review and your personal action plan. It is an important aspect of everyone's training and development to meet regularly and review your progress on an ongoing basis.

When action plans are devised, they plan to take in every aspect of your development, which means an action plan will look into where you were, where you are now and where you want to progress in the future. By gaining this type of information, it will allow you and the person responsible to fit together a history of what you have done previously and how you are performing now.

When the review takes place, you will be able to see how you have progressed. For example, last week you could not demonstrate a specific skill you had planned for; however, this week you demonstrated it to the correct skill level. At the end of a review, you should have identified new action points to help you progress in areas that you are weakest in.

With the person responsible, you will be developing your own action plan which will relate to your performance during the activity session you have assisted with. When you develop this action plan, you will need to bring with you some information to help the person responsible to assess your performance. These pieces of information could include:

- Your activity session plans and risk assessments
- Feedback from the person responsible on how well you did during the emergency procedures
- Feedback from the group, individuals or colleagues
- Footage from videos of the session
- Other review or feedback information from other sources and other people

The person responsible can use this information to assess your strengths and weaknesses and give the review structure.

During your review, the person responsible will focus on your strengths and weaknesses, or on how well you have performed and areas that need further training and development.

Reflecting on performance

The person responsible will usually ask you: how well do think the session went? Do you think the session went well? Were there aspects of the activity session that you feel needed to be improved? Before answering these questions, you may need to think about the activity and the participants:

- Did the participants enjoy the activity?
- Were the course aims met?

- Did you enjoy the activity, and would you change anything next time?
- Were you able to assist the person responsible during the activity that you had planned for?
- Were your explanations and instructions appropriate?
- Were you able to demonstrate the activity?
- What were the two emergencies you had to deal with?
- How well did you cope with the emergency, and would you do anything differently next time?
- Were you able to follow the instructions given to you by the person responsible?
- Did you encounter any problems, and how did you solve them?

With this information, you can assess whether you were able to carry out the tasks that you had planned for at the beginning. By providing this information, the person responsible will be able to give feedback to you on:

- How you were able to plan and carry out risk assessments for the activities
- Your overall performance during the activity session
- How you performed while instructing, explaining and demonstrating aspects of the activity
- How you were able to deal with the different emergencies
- Whether the participant aims were met
- How you planned and prepared yourself for the session.

Top Tip
Prepare yourself for your action plan; remember to take with you the necessary information that will form the basis of your review. You will then be able to complete your action plan.

Top Tip
By reflecting on what you have done, you may find it easier to give examples of your strengths during the activity session and emergency procedures when you have your review with the person responsible.

Development reviews can also highlight any areas in which you may need further training and development. As a result of this, you may be asked to take part in further activity sessions or emergency scenarios in a sport and recreation environment.

Quick Test

1. When should reviews of your training and development take place?

2. What will your action plan relate to?

3. Who will you be having your review with?

4. What can development reviews also highlight?

Answers 1. Regularly. **2.** Your performance during the activity session. **3.** The person responsible. **4.** Areas in which you may need further training and development.

What are daily centre duties?

A realistic working environment

During this Unit, you will be expected to discuss, with the person responsible, your work schedule for the time you are in the 'realistic working environment'. These tasks will include setting up, taking down and storage of equipment, cleaning and tidying of facility areas and responding to client needs. With the person responsible, you will discuss your tasks, and you will need to note down how these tasks are to be carried out – for example, times when equipment needs to be set up, what kind of equipment and maybe how the equipment is set up.

This Unit is designed to enable you to gain practical experience in how different equipment is set up, taken down and stored, as well as ensuring that the facilities are kept clean and tidy. Therefore it is important that you do these tasks with the person responsible at all times.

When assisting with the setting up, taking down and storage of equipment, it is important that you ensure that all aspects of health and safety are followed – for example, moving and handling large pieces of equipment, using appropriate **Personal Protective Equipment (PPE)** and following the centre's procedures at all times.

Dealing with equipment

You will set up equipment by:
- Locating correct equipment for the activity
- Checking equipment for faults, damage or missing parts
- equipment is set up on time for the activity
- Ensuring the equipment is set up safely according to manufacturers' guidelines
- Making reports on unserviceable equipment.

You will take down and store equipment by:
- Dismantling equipment according to the organisation's guidelines
- Identifying any equipment that has been damaged or has missing parts
- Storing it away in its correct location ready to use again
- Ensuring that storage areas are kept clean and tidy
- Removing faulty or damaged equipment
- Completing any relevant reports.

Maintaining facilities

You will also be maintaining facility areas in a supervised role after discussions with the person responsible, by carrying out cleaning and tidying duties according to an agreed daily work schedule. You will need to:

- Clean and tidy areas using the correct PPE and materials
- Follow the organisation's procedures for carrying out any scheduled cleaning and tidying duties
- Know which materials and equipment are used for cleaning and tidying facilities, and identify the appropriate materials for the 'job'
- Correctly deal with and dispose of spillages, breakages and waste
- Ensure that materials are correctly stored in line with organisational and health and safety procedures
- Maintain areas within a centre or organisation to ensure that all emergency exits are kept clear
- Complete any relevant reports and schedules
- Report any problems to the person responsible.

For this Unit, you will learn the basics of health and safety relevant to the setting up and taking down of equipment, basic overview of **COSHH** (Control of Substances Hazardous to Health), a basic manual handling techniques and the correct PPE (Personal Protective Equipment) and equipment for the duties you will be carrying out.

Lastly, while you are carrying out your daily centre duties as discussed with the person responsible, you are expected to assist with any client needs. When clients request your assistance in an enquiry, you will need to respond to the client appropriately and try to assist the client to the best of your ability while ensuring good client relations. You will need to seek help and assistance from others if you cannot deal with the client's needs yourself.

Employability skills in this Unit

In this Unit, you will have the opportunity to develop a range of **employability skills**. These are:

 Awareness of health and safety issues

 Time management

Top Tip
Look out for the symbol to see where the **employability skills** have been covered.

Top Tip
Remember, any words in GREEN are explained in the GLOSSARY section on pages 94–95.

What is an induction?

Orientation

An **induction** is an important aspect of any client or new employee introduction to a centre, facility or organisation. For a client, their induction may be to be shown where:

- relevant facilities are, e.g. toilets
- fire exits are located and what to do in the event of an emergency
- the relevant activity facilities are, e.g. sports hall, swimming pool etc.

An employee induction is used to train a new member of staff and will provide them with the relevant necessary information to carry out their work safely. Most inductions are recorded formally, and both the new member of staff and their inductor (normally their supervisor) will sign and date the induction record to confirm that they have covered each important aspect of their induction. The time it takes to complete an induction will vary, and will all depend on the tasks to be carried out as part of the job.

Different types of induction

Inductions may be split up into different categories: personnel, health and safety, and site-specific. The content of an induction form will vary in each centre or organisation, but may include the following.

Personnel induction may include:

- Completion of personnel details – for example, name, address, emergency contact information etc.
- Issue and explanations of job description, hours of work, work duties, company policies and procedures
- Introduction to supervisor and other colleagues
- Issue of staff uniform.

Health and safety induction may include:

- Employee reading the company's health and safety policy, including rules and procedures for all aspects of health and safety – for example, risk assessments, manual handling, COSHH, RIDDOR etc.
- Emergency procedures – for example, fire-exit routes, first-aid facilities
- The company's policies and procedures for child protection
- Correct use of uniform and different types of PPE they may need to wear, and their location.

Site-specific inductions may include:

- Areas where the employee will be working
- What equipment they will be using
- Specific health and safety issues relating to activity equipment and facilities.

Health and safety for you and others

By law, all organisations and activity centres will have produced guidelines for their staff on how they conduct themselves when dealing with equipment (whether this is setting up, taking down or storing equipment). This is because they need to ensure that their staff comply with these guidelines in order to protect anyone who uses the equipment (staff and clients).

Before anyone is allowed to deal with any piece of equipment, all members of staff will have taken part in an induction where they will have been shown how to set up and take down the equipment correctly. During this induction, they may be shown how to look for faults or damage which would make the equipment unserviceable and potentially dangerous for clients using the facility.

The guidelines are also in place to ensure the safety of client groups using the centre's equipment, and therefore the centre has a **duty of care** over the clients who use their facilities. Failure to look after and keep clients safe from harm could be construed as **negligence**.

Health and safety training

When you are dealing with equipment in a facility, you will be working with the **person responsible** when you are being trained and while you are carrying out agreed duties that involve the setting up, taking down and storing of equipment.

Examples of the kind of health and safety training you should receive when dealing with equipment are:

- Knowing how to set up and take down equipment according to organisational procedures
- Checking equipment for damage, faults and missing parts
- Correct handling of equipment
- Dealing with damaged equipment and completing the correct reports.

Top Tip
It is important that you complete your induction in full. Try not to miss anything out, as this will prevent you from carrying out your duties.

Top Tip
Find out from the person responsible what the guidelines are in your centre for dealing with equipment.

Quick Test

1. When would you receive an induction?

2. What are the three main types of induction you may receive?

3. What does the centre have a duty of care over?

4. Who will make sure that you receive health and safety training in the centre?

Answers **1.** When you are new to the centre, facility or organisation. **2.** Personnel, health and safety and site-specific. **3.** Anyone that uses the centre. **4.** The person responsible.

Working to a schedule

The schedule log

In this Unit, you will be expected to assist the person responsible in carrying out a range of tasks that involve equipment and facilities which you will agree with the person responsible. This list of tasks or jobs may need to be done at a specific time or throughout your time in the centre.

Your assessment form for 'logging' these tasks consists of two pages. On the first page, you will be expected to work with the person responsible to agree the tasks in which you will be involved in the facilities. This schedule log will contain:

- The time when the tasks have to be carried out by, and how long you have to complete them
- What the task is, for example, setting up equipment for an activity
- Sections for you and the person responsible to sign when the work has been carried out.

Task No.	Time	Task	Candidate signature	Person responsible signature
1	9.00am	Clean and tidy changing room areas, before 9.30am		
2	10.00am	Set up kayaks and paddles for group of 8, before 10.30am		
3	2.00pm	Take down badminton equipment, by 2.30pm		
4	2.30pm	Tidy entrance area and empty bins		

There may be occasions where additional daily routine tasks will also have to be completed over and above the daily schedule for that day.

5	Empty bins and dispose of rubbish around the centre		
6	Tidy entrance hall and update any promotional material		

On the second page, there is a 'candidate's notes' section for you to note down how these tasks are to be completed, what equipment you will need, what PPE to wear etc. This is designed to help you remember what you need to do when you and the person responsible agree on the scheduled tasks.

Task No.	Notes
1	Equipment: key to cleaning cupboard, mop and bucket, PPE: gloves, plastic apron. Speak to person responsible to mix the cleaning chemicals with water for correct dilution.
2	Speak to colleague for help taking kayaks down off storage racks and lift to edge of the loch. Take out 7 junior paddles and 1 adult paddle and place one by each kayak.

Carrying out scheduled duties

Being in the correct location, at the correct time

When undertaking tasks detailed in the centre or organisation, it is important that you use your time efficiently and plan when tasks need to be completed. This requires you to manage your time. It can feel like you have to juggle tasks around so that you can complete the tasks. With practice, you should become efficient, which will ensure that the tasks are completed.

For example: You have planned your schedule for the day and agreed the particular tasks and any routine tasks that you will be assisting the person responsible with. (See the first two tables on the opposite page.)

The first table shows you that certain tasks have to be carried out at specific times, i.e. *"Clean and tidy changing-room areas, before 9:30am"*, or *"Take down badminton equipment, by 2:30pm"*. The reason this has to happen is that:

- Centre has to be clean and tidy for clients before the centre opens
- Activities are due to begin at a certain time
- Another activity that is using the same facility (i.e. sports hall) may have to be set up straight after.

Completing the notes section on the second page (see bottom table on the opposite page) will help you to organise yourself by making notes about what equipment, help, and so on, you may need.

Managing your time around these set tasks will allow you to 'fit in' those other routine tasks. From the first table, you can see that there are one to three hours between the start of one set task and another, which means that would be the ideal time to carry out the daily routine tasks. (See second table on the opposite page.)

13

T☼p Tip
Always talk through your schedule log with the person responsible. Anything you do not understand or are unable to do can be dealt with.

T☼p Tip
You will need to plan and organise your time to be able to carry out scheduled tasks on time.

T☼p Tip
Find out how your daily routine tasks can be fitted in to *your* schedule log.

T☼p Tip
Work with the person responsible and find out what your tasks are.

✎ Quick Test

1. With whom should you be discussing what your scheduled tasks are?

2. On your scheduled task list, what information will you need to record other than what the specified task is?

3. What must you plan efficiently in order to complete the scheduled tasks?

4. What can you use to make notes on about your scheduled tasks?

Answers 1. The person responsible. 2. The time it has to be done by. 3. Your time. 4. Candidate's notes section.

Setting up and taking down equipment

First steps

For your assessment, you will be assisting the person responsible to set up and take down equipment, and it will be important that you follow all health and safety procedures at all times.

Do I need help? You will need to consider that larger or heavier equipment may need more than one person to move it into its correct location. In some cases, larger or heavier equipment may have its own specialist piece of equipment to lift, push, pull etc. into position, for example, a trolley. If you have any doubt, ask the person responsible.

Setting up equipment

When setting up equipment, it is important that:

- **It is set up in the correct location.** For example, some centres use sports halls for different types of activities, and as a result the floor will be marked for multiple activities, for example, basketball, tennis, football etc. If you are setting up for a badminton session, make sure that the net is set on the lines marked for badminton!

- **It is set up at the correct time**. Equipment is usually set up *BEFORE* an activity session begins, especially if it involves larger pieces of equipment. Therefore it is important that, if the task is to set up equipment for an *activity that begins* at 10:30am, the equipment must be set up before this time in order for the *activity to start on time*.

Taking down equipment

Points to consider when taking down equipment:

- **Be on time.** If your schedule is to take down equipment at a specific time, this is usually because there could be a different activity using the sports hall immediately afterwards.

- **Adhere to manufacturers' and centre guidelines.** Make sure that you take down equipment safely. This is for your safety and for that of others.

Safe storage of equipment

For health and safety reasons, it is important that all storage areas are kept in a clean and tidy condition. Also consider how you put away equipment in a store to ensure that accessibility and safety are maintained at all times.

Good examples

A good example of a store:

- Clearly labelled areas for sports equipment – this helps with storing equipment in specific places for each sport

- Separate areas for every sporting equipment – this way it will be easy to retrieve sports equipment for the next session without spending time trying to find all the necessary pieces

- Large or heavy equipment on floor level – the equipment will be easer to retrieve and will be safer than placing it up high where it may do harm by falling

- Small items bagged or boxed up – this will keep storage areas clear of equipment and easier to retrieve. As a safety point, by keeping small items bagged/boxed, it will prevent someone falling over

- Access in and out kept clear – this will enable you to get in and out of the storage area, but it will also enable you to remove or store equipment more easily, and will ensure the safety of anyone who enters the store

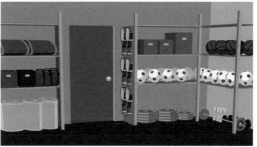

- Clean equipment – this is always good practice, when setting up equipment and storing equipment always clean the equipment ready for the next session. By cleaning equipment you may find if there are any breakages or faults with the equipment that you may have missed before!

Bad examples

The list above showed you what a store should look like. A **bad example of a store** would have:

- Dirty equipment
- Items of equipment stored everywhere
- Access in and out restricted
- Large or heavy items not secured and stored high
- Equipment stored wherever there is a space!

Top Tip
Ask the person responsible how different items of equipment should be stored in your facility.

Top Tip
To find out when equipment has to be set up and taken down, look at your schedule log.

✎ Quick Test

1. What will you need to do if you have to set up large or heavy pieces of equipment?

2. What two aspects will you need to consider when taking down equipment?

3. For health and safety reasons, what state must the store be kept in?

4. What must you ensure when you store equipment?

Answers 1. Ask for help from others. **2.** Be on time and adhere to manufacturers'/centre guidelines. **3.** A clean and tidy state. **4.** Accessibility and safety are maintained at all times.

Manual handling

Introduction to manual handling

The "**Manual Handling Operations Regulations**" 1992 (which were amended in 2002) cover a wide range of activities that involve lifting, carrying, pushing, pulling or lowering. What this means is that there are regulations that employers, trainers, etc. have to comply with to ensure the safety of themselves, their staff, students or clients. This is to prevent them hurting themselves while they carry out work duties or while participating on activities. If you are unsure if you need assistance with a piece of equipment – ask the person responsible!

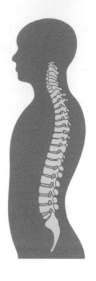

How will this affect me?

Before you begin to move any type of equipment, you will be given training by the person responsible in how to do this safely. By not following the procedures and the training you have been given about how to handle heavy, awkward or large objects, you may injure yourself. The most common injury, for people who do not follow the procedures or the training they have been given, is to their back (or more accurately their spine).

These injuries could be: strained muscles, spinal discs being moved out of place, inflamed muscles around the spine, or sciatica (injury to a nerve from the back that runs down the leg through the buttock).

How can we prevent injury?

To prevent injuries from happening, it is important that you take part in training, follow any guidelines that manufacturers give on handling the equipment, and follow any centre/organisations policies and procedures.

1.
Think before you lift or handle anything.

2.
Get into a stable position – feet apart, one leg slightly forward to keep your balance.

3.
Get yourself into a good posture.

4.
Make sure that the object you are lifting/carrying is held close to your waist.

Do look where you are going.

Don't look down and away from where you are going.

Do stop to rest or adjust your hand position before continuing.

Do keep your body straight and in line with the object you are carrying.

Don't twist your back or lean sideways (especially if you are bent over).

How will this apply to activity equipment?

If you were asked to set up equipment for:

Cricket: The equipment you had to set up is: stumps, bats and leg padding.

The equipment is light and easy for one person to set up.

Canoeing: The equipment you had to remove from store: four canoes.

The canoes are heavy, therefore it is necessary that two or more people carry them to set them up.

If you do have to move, lift or pull any types of equipment, it is important that you follow the few simple steps below:

1 Look at the task to be done

Will it involve lifting heavy equipment or carrying equipment over long distances? You may need to revise how you transport the equipment. Consider getting help or using trolleys or other devices designed to do the job.

2 What will you be carrying?

Will the equipment be heavy, difficult to grasp, loaded awkwardly? Consider reducing the amount you carry or use other devices that are designed to do the job.

3 Where are you going?

Where are you transporting equipment? Will the floor/ground be slippery or uneven, or will there be difficult weather conditions? Consider wearing appropriate PPE, and perhaps alternative venues. If alternative venues cannot be found, help and assistance will need to be found.

Top Tip
It is important to assess what you need to be lifting or moving – this way you will prevent injury.

Top Tip
What types of equipment will you be handling – do you need one person to set up and take down the equipment, or many people?

Quick Test

1. When were the "Manual Handling Operations Regulations" amended?

2. What is the most common injury sustained by people who have moved heavy or awkward objects?

3. How can you prevent further injury from happening when moving heavy or awkward objects?

4. What are the three important steps to moving heavy or awkward objects?

Answers 1. 2002. **2.** Their back or spine. **3.** Take part in training, and follow the centre's guidelines and policies/procedures. **4.** Look at the task to be done. What you will be carrying and where you are going.

Personal protective equipment

The importance of personal protective equipment

When you are carrying out scheduled cleaning and tidying duties or other duties in the facility, such as setting up and taking down equipment, you have to ensure that you have the correct Personal Protective Equipment (PPE).

It is a regulation under the "Personal Protective Equipment at Work Regulations" 1992 that all organisations should provide adequate protective equipment for all staff and users of their facility. The centre has to ensure that:

- Checks are done to determine PPEs' suitability
- The equipment has regular checks to determine that it is maintained and that PPE is stored appropriately and in the correct place
- Training and instructions are given to the users of PPE to ensure that they know how to wear it correctly.

What is PPE?

All users of a sport and recreation facility will wear some form of PPE at all times when they carry out specific tasks. Below are examples of the types of PPE that you may use, for different parts of the body:

	Examples of hazards that may occur in the centre	Examples of the types of PPE that can be used
Head	Impact from falling or flying objects, risk of head bumping, hair entanglement	A range of helmets and bump caps, nets to keep hair from getting tangled
Eyes	Chemical splash, dust, projectiles, gas and vapour, radiation (i.e. sunburn)	Safety spectacles, goggles, face shields, visors, masks
Breathing	Dust, vapour, gas, oxygen-deficient atmospheres	Disposable filtering facepiece or respirator
Whole body	Temperature extremes, adverse weather, chemical splash, spray from pressure leaks or spray guns, impact or penetration, contaminated dust, excessive wear or entanglement of own clothing	Conventional or disposable overalls, boiler suits, specialist protective clothing, e.g. high-visibility clothing
Hands and arms	Abrasion, temperature extremes, cuts and punctures, impact, chemicals, electric shock, skin infection, disease or contamination	Gloves, gauntlets, mitts, wrist cuffs, armlets
Feet and legs	Wet, electrostatic build-up, slipping, cuts and punctures, falling objects, chemical splash, abrasion	Safety boots and shoes with protective toe caps and penetration-resistant mid-sole, gaiters, leggings, spats

Task-related PPE

Staff uniforms

These will generally consist of a T-shirt, trousers or shorts, and these items of clothing will also have the company logo. Uniforms also allow clients to know who the members of staff are.

Cleaning and tidying PPE

This may include items such as gloves, apron, boots, goggles, etc. You will find that, depending on the task, there may be specific items of PPE you will need to wear for a certain task. You may be required to wear more or fewer items of PPE than are listed above or opposite.

Setting up, taking down and storing equipment

This kind of PPE can be quite varied. Usually, most people will wear their uniform, however, there may be occasions when you need to wear more items of PPE. Here are a few examples:

- when you are outside – weather conditions will need to be taken into account, therefore warm and/or waterproof jackets may need to be worn

- when working in confined spaces – a helmet may need to be worn

- working near traffic or in poor daylight, (e.g. during winter months) high-visibility jackets may need to be worn.

MIND YOUR HEAD

Top Tip
Always check with the person responsible what PPE you will need to wear for the scheduled tasks you will be doing.

Top Tip
You will receive training on the types of PPE you will be using for your scheduled tasks.

✎ Quick Test

1. When must you wear PPE?

2. What is PPE?

3. Give an example of PPE that can be worn on your head.

4. Give an example of PPE that can be worn over your mouth and nose.

Answers 1. When you are carrying out any scheduled tasks. **2.** Protective equipment that organisations must provide to ensure the safety of users. **3.** Helmet or net. **4.** Disposable face mask or respirator.

Using correct materials when cleaning and tidying

Policies and procedures

Every centre or organisation will have its own policies and procedures drawn up for their staff to comply with whenever they carry out any duties that require cleaning and tidying. When you carry out these duties, you will be given training on what types of equipment are to be used and where to use them.

Your course tutor or the person responsible will ensure that all the necessary aspects of cleaning and tidying are covered, such as:

- what tasks need to be done according to the agreed schedule – these could be cleaning the changing-room areas, sports hall etc.
- what PPE you will need – gloves, plastic aprons, boots etc.
- dealing with spillages, breakages and waste – how to deal with these safely and using the correct equipment to deal with them
- storage of cleaning equipment – tidily, and ensuring that it is put away in the correct storage area to avoid contamination
- completing any relevant reports.

To be able to do the above tasks, you will need to know where and what kind of equipment you may need to complete the job. In most centres and organisations, cleaning and tidying equipment, for example, mops and buckets, will be colour-coded:

RED	BLUE
Bathroom and sanitary areas – e.g. toilets, urinals, showers etc.	Bathroom and sanitary areas – e.g. toilets, urinals, showers etc.

GREEN	YELLOW
General areas and bars – e.g. dining room, cafés etc.	Wash basins and other washroom surfaces – e.g. sinks, tiles etc.

These colour-coded pieces of equipment will also be stored in separate areas and used in their specific areas to ensure that there is no cross-contamination from one area to another, for example, from public toilets to kitchen areas.

Dealing with spillages and breakages

All centres will have a procedure on how to deal with spillages and breakages. When you are informed that a spillage or a breakage has taken place, make sure you inform the person responsible and assist them with dealing with the incident. This would involve making sure that you have the correct PPE and cleaning materials.

It is important you make sure that, when dealing with any spillages and breakages, you follow the centre's guidelines at all times and the appropriate signage is put up informing people of the hazard to ensure that it does not cause an accident – for example, people slipping or cutting themselves.

The types of **spillages** you may encounter are:

- From drinks, e.g. juice, fizzy drinks
- From body fluids, e.g. blood, urine (see below)
- Spillages found in sports areas, e.g. water on a swimming pool side, leaks from windows

The types of **breakages** you may encounter are:

- From broken equipment, for example:
  - Sports equipment – goal nets
  - Safety equipment – throw lines (pool)
- From broken areas within the facility, for example (see below):
  - Window glass
  - Bottles
  - Chairs

STOP!!!

At all times, you must follow the centre's health and safety policies and procedures before you go to clean or tidy up spillages or breakages. The reasons are that there could be a health risk to you or anyone else - for example, if the spillage is blood, urine or any other type of body fluid, cross-contamination could take place.

Another hazard you will need to watch out for is "sharps". Where something is broken, you may need to consider your health and safety in dealing with these items – for example, broken glass or other sharp objects. However, sharps may also include items such as needles and syringes. If you find any of these items, **DO NOT** deal with them yourself – inform the person responsible **IMMEDIATELY**!

IF IN DOUBT, SPEAK TO THE PERSON RESPONSIBLE!

Top Tip
If you are unsure what equipment to use – ASK!

Top Tip
Ask the person responsible how you are to deal with any spillages and breakages.

Quick Test

1. What are the four colours used to code cleaning and tidying equipment?

2. Why do centres use different colours for different facilities?

3. What must you do if a spillage or a breakage has taken place?

4. What must you do if you come across any "sharps"?

Answers 1. Red, blue, green and yellow. **2.** To avoid cross-contamination. **3.** Inform the person responsible. **4.** Do not deal with it alone, but inform the person responsible immediately.

COSHH

COSHH

In a working environment, where any type of hazardous substance is used or is present, for example, swimming-pool chemicals, washing-up liquid, floor cleaner, toilet cleaner, dust and so on, it is the law that all organisations and centres will have to comply with a set of Regulations called **COSHH**, which stands for:

Control

Of

Substances

Hazardous to

Health

These Regulations are to protect employers, staff, clients and anyone else who may be exposed to **hazardous substances**. A hazardous substance can make someone ill, if the person has:

- **Ingested** – by swallowing
- **Inhaled** – breathing in by fumes (smoke, airborne particles)
- **Absorbed** – through the skin (this may be a liquid, powder, cream or gel-like substance)
- **Injected** – through the skin straight into the body via sharp objects such as needle.

What substances are covered by COSHH?

COSHH Regulations will cover most of the substances you will come into contact with, for example, cleaning agents. But what else does COSHH cover?

- Dusty environments
- Where you may have to mix chemicals, e.g. when diluting cleaning chemicals into water (water is also a substance that can react badly with a 'chemical')
- Any other substances that is a risk to health and that may be found in the centre

And it **does not** cover:

- Any biological agents outside the centre's control, for example, catching colds or viruses from other people using the facility or employees
- Asbestos or lead – you may only encounter this if you are in an old building where asbestos had been used for roofing or insulating pipes, or lead is present in old piping or some types of paint
- Substances that are radioactive or have explosive or flammable properties.

COSHH Regulations

COSHH Regulations make sure that centres and organisations put the following policies and procedures in place and make sure that they adhere to them:

- Assess the hazard, minimise the risk and put control measures in place

- Make sure the staff with an organisation or centre are trained appropriately to deal with and handle hazardous substances
- Ensure that staff training is carried out, recorded and kept up to date
- Make provisions for Personal Protective Equipment for all members of staff
- Make sure that staff wear the appropriate Personal Protective Equipment
- Have plans and procedures in place to deal with accidents and emergencies.

Dos and Don'ts

DO

- Wear Personal Protective Equipment when dealing with any cleaning chemicals
- Use the correct chemicals for the task
- Always read the label and follow the instructions
- Always put up signs or notices indicating what you are doing (e.g. 'Slippery floor' signs etc.)

DON'T

- Mix any chemicals – always ask the person responsible if you are unsure about anything
- Use any containers for the tasks – instead, use the appropriate materials for the task
- Use undiluted chemicals – some chemicals may be used undiluted, but always read the label and follow the instructions

COSHH data sheets

COSHH data sheets are pages of information that arrive with any consignment of chemicals or are printed directly on the container come from the manufacturer. These data sheets will give information about:

- The name of the chemical
- How it is to be stored
- A risk assessment on its contents: whether it will give off fumes or ignite in certain conditions (e.g. reaction to water), what the hazard will be if it comes in contact with, for example, skin
- How to use it (e.g. dilute with water)
- How the chemical is to be disposed of
- What Personal Protective Equipment must be worn
- What to do in emergencies, i.e. fire, spillages etc.
- What you must do in a first-aid situation, i.e. if the chemical is inhaled or swallowed, comes in contact with your eyes or skin etc.

Top Tip
COSHH should be part of your induction into the centre, and should be covered before you carry out any cleaning and tidying tasks.

Top Tip
Always make sure that you abide by COSHH Regulations and wear the appropriate PPE.

Quick Test

1. What does COSHH stand for?
2. What does absorbed mean?
3. Why were COSHH Regulations put in place?
4. What are COSHH data sheets?

Answers 1. Control of Substances Hazardous to Health 2. Through the skin. 3. To make sure centre users are protected and safe from hazardous substances. 4. Information about the chemical that has come directly from the manufacturer.

Correct storage of cleaning and tidying materials

Store rooms

Store rooms for cleaning and tidying materials should be kept in the same condition: safe, clean and tidy! The person responsible will be able to show you where they should be kept and how to store them safely, and staff should have access to the necessary personal protective equipment before they use any cleaning and tidying equipment and materials.

When you are carrying out the agreed duties with the person responsible, you will need to make sure that the cleaning and tidying store is:

- clean – this will prevent cleaning and tidying equipment from getting cross-contaminated by other cleaning products
- stored tidily – this will ensure that the cleaning and tidying equipment is easily found when it is needed next
- stored safely – to prevent staff from having any accidents
- locked – this will prevent unauthorised users from having access to the equipment, for example, children.

The main difference with cleaning and tidying materials is that there are guidelines set out by the manufacturers on how you must store their materials. When storing certain cleaning chemicals, it is very important that they are stored according to the procedures laid down by the centre and by the manufacturer of the chemical. This is because some chemicals may react to each other, which will cause serious problems, for example, giving off toxic vapours.

Unlike activity equipment, cleaning and tidying materials cannot be stored in the same store. In a centre there are different facilities, for example, toilets, showers, reception, kitchens, staff facilities. As a result, in some centres they will have certain types of cleaning materials that have to be stored in different places to avoid contamination from the different facilities, therefore centres and organisations may have adopted the use of different coloured cleaning materials, e.g. anything that is coloured green = kitchen, red = changing rooms etc.

When you go to store the equipment, you will have to ensure that it is ready for future use.

Keeping facility areas safe

To maintain areas in a safe and tidy condition, you will have to ensure that any incidents are dealt with quickly and efficiently without disturbing staff and clients who are using the facility while keeping them safe from harm.

Spillages, breakages or waste must be dealt with according to the centre's procedures, by using the correct equipment and PPE for the task and seeking advice from the person responsible. The person responsible will also be able to help you with these agreed tasks and provide training and guidance on how to deal with these types of incidents.

The centre will have carried out a risk assessment on the hazards for spillages, breakageS and the disposal of waste. As a result of this risk assessment, certain control measures will have been agreed; training will have taken place for staff to ensure that the risks are reduced for all users at the centre.

In order to keep all users at the centre safe, you may be asked to use a variety of methods to direct them away from harm. These could be:

- Signage – posters (area out of use/bounds)
- Warning tape – used to mark off dangerous or hazardous areas
- Floor signs – "slippery floor" signs

While you are carrying out your agreed working schedule, you will be expected to ensure that the facility areas are kept in a safe and tidy condition. What this means is that, when you go about the tasks that you agreed with the person responsible, you will have to ensure that any entrances, exits and emergency exits are kept clear and unobstructed.

As fire exits are not used regularly, these areas may have been used to store items temporarily. It is important, if you find this happening, to report it to the person responsible.

It is also important to check the outside of the facility, especially the outsides of fire exits. Look out for rubbish, misplaced bins etc. that could prevent the doors from opening. If this happens, inform the person responsible and follow their instructions.

Top Tip
Most store rooms will be set out according to COSHH regulations and manufacturers' data sheet information. If you are unsure where anything is kept, ask the person responsible.

Top Tip
All centres will have hazard warning information. You will need to find out what is used at your facility, as it can vary from one centre to another.

Top Tip
Make sure you follow the facility's guidelines for the storage of cleaning and tidying materials!

Quick Test

1. How should cleaning stores be kept?
2. Can all cleaning and tidying equipment and materials for the entire facility be stored in the same place?
3. Name three different examples to inform staff and clients of a spillage or that something has been broken.
4. What could obstruct and block a fire exit from outside?

Answers 1. Clean, tidy and locked. 2. No. 3. Signage, warning tape and floor signs. 4. rubbish, misplaced bins etc.

Dealing with customer needs

Types of communication

Communication is how we interact with others by using different techniques to achieve our goals of giving and receiving information.

Communication is used every day for a variety of reasons, such as exchanging information with customers or colleagues, when attending an interview or when you are just chatting with your friends. There are three main ways in which we communicate:

- verbal
- written
- body language

Verbal communication

This type of communication is where we convey information with others by talking.

Talking to people	Face to face	Welcoming a customer Communicating with colleagues In a job interview
Using communication devices	Telephones Hand-held radio Intercom	Talking to customers Relaying information to colleagues

Written communication

This type of communication is used when we have to correspond with others by means of writing or drawing.

Examples of written communication:	How ...	When ...
Writing	Notes Memos Letters	Informing colleagues of incidents Passing information on to colleagues who are not on duty at the same time as you
Drawing	Diagrams of facilities Symbols for objects	Carrying out a risk assessment Hazard warning signs

Body language

Types of **body language** are where we unconsciously communicate through the use of postures, gestures or facial expressions. Examples of these are:

Posture:

- Sitting in a chair: a) slumped to one side, resting on the arm of the chair, could mean that you are not interested; b) sitting up, hands on your lap, could mean you are interested in what is going on.

Gesture:

- Putting your hand to your cheek could mean you are thinking about something.
- Tapping or drumming fingers could mean you are impatient.

Facial expressions:

- Smiling or frowning could give the other person a clear idea what you are thinking. Facial expressions are probably the easiest form of body language you can recognise.

Another way in which body language is used for communication is through signing for people who have difficulty hearing. This is called **sign language**.

Here are some examples of sign language:

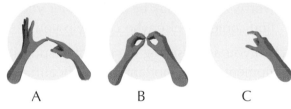

A   B   C

Recording client interactions

For your assessment, you will have to record the customer interactions you have had in the facility. You will need to give information about:

- what the interaction with the client was – for example, was it an enquiry about what the facility offers, or directions to the fitness suite?
- whether you were able to deal with the client's requests or needs
- whether you asked for help or assistance to deal with the client's requests or needs – for example, you were unsure where the fitness suite was, but by asking a colleague you were able to direct the client
- what instructions you gave to the client - for example, after finding out where the fitness suite was, you were able to find the facility.

Top Tip
Learn the different types of communication.

Top Tip
Learn how you would communicate with customers in an organisation/ centre.

Quick Test

1. What are the three main forms of communication?
2. Name two types of written communication.
3. How would you communicate through body language?
4. How could people who have difficulty in hearing communicate?

Answers 1. Verbal, written and body language. **2.** Writing or drawing. **3.** Use of posture, gesture and facial expressions. **4.** By sign language.

Seeking help and assistance

Everyone who works in a sport and recreation facility will at some point need help and assistance with their tasks and duties. This help and assistance is not intended for others to do your work for you, but to allow you carry out your scheduled tasks and duties that otherwise you may be unable to complete.

When will I need help?

When you need help and assistance, it is important that you ask for it in a way that is appropriate. This means that you need to be polite to the person you are asking, and be clear about what it is you want them to do – for example:

- Explain what the task is that you need help with.
- Give an estimate of how long it will take (don't worry if you don't know) – a five-minute task most people will assist you with, but a 30-minute task could cause you problems, as other people will have their own tasks and duties for the day and may be unable to help you at this time. If this is the case, don't worry, as they may be able to refer you to someone else, or you may need to find someone else who can help you.

When you are assisting the person responsible to set up and take down equipment, it is important that all health and safety procedures are followed at all times. Certain members of staff may be unable to give you help and assistance for this because they may have sustained an injury to their back.

Do I need help?

Bear in mind that larger or heavier pieces of equipment may need more than one person to move into position – *planning is essential* for this, as you will be taking people away from their work! Some larger or heavier equipment may have its own specialist piece of equipment to move it into position, for example, a trolley. If you have any doubt, ask the person responsible.

Completion of reports and reporting

Set procedures

In centres, there will be set procedures that staff will have to follow when dealing with problems they may have with pieces of equipment. It is important that you report anything you find wrong with a piece of equipment and that you also follow the centre's procedures. There are different ways in which we can report:

- **Verbally**: to the person responsible or manager
- **Written**: in the centre's equipment log.

1/8/07	2:00pm	Broken mirror in female changing area – area clear of glass, and glass disposed of safely – mirror to be replaced
5/8/07	4:00pm	2 × kayak carrying handles are missing – need to be replaced
10/8/07	10:00am	1 × small waterproof trouser bottoms have a hole in the knee – need to be repaired
27/8/07	10:00am	Cleaning chemical leaking in store cupboard – informed person responsible

Usually, if you have to report that a piece of equipment is damaged, faulty or has missing parts, the items are removed immediately from the store and placed into a separate area designated specially for this use. If the centre does not have a separate area, they mark the equipment in some way to highlight to others that a particular piece of equipment is not to be used.

By removing these unusable items from the normal store, you are ensuring that these items will not be used until they are fixed or the items have been replaced, as this could be dangerous for clients and staff on their next activity session.

Remember that, when you are dealing with cleaning and tidying materials (see example in table above), and where chemicals are involved, you must ensure that you inform the person responsible as soon as possible and follow their instructions and the information detailed on the COSHH data sheets at all times.

Top Tip
Do not be afraid to ask for help or assistance from anyone. Colleagues may not necessarily be able to help you all the time, but may offer alternatives instead.

Top Tip
When you find a piece of equipment that is unserviceable, always ask the advice of the person responsible before taking any action yourself.

Top Tip
Ask the person responsible where the equipment goes if it is faulty, is damaged or has missing parts.

Quick Test

1. When might you need help and assistance from others?

2. Why would you need help and assistance when setting up or taking down equipment?

3. Name two kinds of reports.

4. When may you have to complete a report when you are completing your scheduled tasks?

Answers 1. When carrying out scheduled work duties. **2.** The equipment could be heavy or awkward. **3.** Verbal and written. **4.** If a piece of equipment is damaged, faulty or has missing parts.

Identification of career pathways

Career pathways

There are many pathways to gaining a career in sport and recreation. A career pathway is a route you will take over a long period of time, possibly a lifetime, to gain the necessary skills, qualifications and experience to achieve your goal. What your goal is will determine what kind of career you wish to embark upon.

From school, you will begin to learn about what opportunities there are and to start the process of choosing a pathway that will enable you to focus on what training, assessment and experiences you need to obtain, which will ultimately result in you gaining employment.

This process is what is called lifelong learning, where we continuously keep up to date with skills and qualifications. This will also include training for a higher level of skill and qualifications. Different pathways will determine what kinds of skills and qualifications we gain, whether we go down the academic pathway which will lead us to college and university, or directly into vocational training in a workplace. Whichever pathway we choose, we end up in the same place: employment.

There is a huge selection of opportunities for people wishing to follow a career in sport and recreation. Below are a few examples:

Leisure/sports centre	Pool lifeguard, gym instructor, activities coach, sports development officer, centre manager
Outdoor centre	Activity instructor/coach, senior instructor, centre manager

Where can I find career information?

The person responsible should be able to assist you with gaining information on where to find out about career information. There are huge resources available that you should be able to access and gather information from. The list below will give you an idea of what is out there and what kind of information you will find in each of the resources:

- Newspapers – these have information on opportunities locally and nationally.

- College prospectuses – will give you information on how you can gain higher-level academic qualifications in sport and recreation, for example sports science, sports development, fitness health and exercise etc.

- The Jobcentre Plus – job centres (which you can now access on the Internet) are able to provide information on jobs locally and nationally. They can also provide information on vocational training courses, for example, Skillseekers and Modern Apprenticeship schemes.

- Industry magazines – these offer one of the best resources for information in your chosen pathway. They will give information about what kinds of jobs are on offer, the kinds of qualifications, skills and experience needed, and what training and assessment courses are on offer.

- Local sport and recreation facilities – these can give you an insight into what kinds of opportunities are on offer, and their staff can give you valuable information on training and assessment courses. The staff may also be able to assist you by telling you what skills, qualifications and experience you will need to gain employment in sport and recreation centres.

- Searching sport and recreation centre recruitment websites – this can be useful, as it will give information on the different types of jobs in the sport and recreation industry and on the different skills, qualifications and experience needed.

- ILAM (Institute of Leisure and Amenities Management) – represents every aspect of leisure, cultural and recreation management and is committed to the improvement of management standards. On their website, they provide information on training and sector resources.

- ISRM (Institute of Sport and Recreation Management) – national professional body for those involved exclusively in providing, managing, operating and developing sport and recreation services in the United Kingdom. They provide information on education and training.

- SkillsActive (Sector Skills Council for Sport and Recreation website) – provides information about training, education and qualifications, and ensures that the National Occupational Standards are kept up to date.

- National governing body websites – they will provide specific information about their sport and opportunities for training and assessment qualifications.

Top Tip
Ask the person responsible what possible career opportunities are available to you.

Top Tip
Most of the career information you should be able to find in the list; however, you may need to seek permission to use the Internet, intranet systems etc.

Quick Test

1. Where will you be able to start to learn about career opportunities?

2. What is lifelong learning?

3. Who can help you obtain information about career opportunities?

4. What information can local papers/newspapers give you on career opportunities?

Answers 1. From school. **2.** A process where we continuously keep up to date with our skills, experiences and qualifications, with progression to a higher level. **3.** The person responsible. **4.** Information on opportunities locally and nationally.

Skills, qualifications and experience needed

Different opportunities will require you to have different skills, qualifications and experience. These will vary from one opportunity to the next, and within the opportunities. For example, in the table below, the 'Sports coach' career opportunity: the industry requirements state that it is for a football coach, where in other opportunities it may state another type of sport, e.g. hockey. When compiling a list of career opportunities, it may be best to separate what the requirements are. The table below gives a few examples of the different types of career opportunities available and how they can be split up to show what skills, qualifications and experience are needed:

Career opportunity	Skills, qualifications and experience needed
Higher/further education, university	• Candidates will need to contact their college or university for more information on the recommended entry levels, as these vary from one establishment to another.
Skillseekers and Modern Apprenticeships	• Skillseekers – no formal entry requirements; candidates have to be between the ages of 16 and 19. Will help you train to a nationally recognised standard and to train for a job through work experience. • Modern apprenticeships – no formal entry requirements, but employees need to demonstrate to their employer that they have the potential to complete the programme.
Leisure attendant	• RLSS National Pool Lifeguard Qualification. • You will require good customer service skills. • Successful applicants are required to provide a CRB enhanced disclosure. • You will be responsible under the guidance of the duty manager for the effective operation of the facility. • Your role will require you to provide lifeguard cover for public and school sessions; setting up and de-rigging equipment; housekeeping duties to include cleaning; safety checks; security; supervision of parties.
(Indoor) climbing instructor	• To be responsible for inspiring and motivating customers. You will help people of all ages, backgrounds and experience levels to develop their confidence through climbing, and will be responsible for promoting a safe climbing environment for experienced and novice climbers alike. • The successful candidate will have good communication skills, relevant personal climbing experience, experience of teaching others and up-to-date knowledge of current climbing best practice, current first aid certificate and Single Pitch Award.
(Football) sports coach	• Duties will include the delivery of coaching sessions for primary school children; assisting with coach training programme. • Candidates must possess an FA coaching qualification, be licensed members of FACA and have, or be willing to obtain, the necessary CRB enhanced disclosure. • Additional national governing body coaching qualifications an advantage.

Do you know your employability skills?

The main feature of Skills for Work courses is the unique way in which they incorporate **employability skills** into all the sport and recreation Units. You will find that you use employability skills every day, sometimes without knowing that you are doing so, by completing set tasks given to you by the person responsible in leisure centres, gyms, outdoor centres etc.

In the Intermediate 2 Skills for Work course, there are 13 employability skills that are assessed. Believe it or not, you will have used all of these skills over and over again at some point every week. Have a look at the table below and see if you can match the examples given to your own weekly activities:

Employability skill	How you may have used them in everyday activities
1. Working co-operatively with others	When you are working with others to achieve a common goal, e.g. putting up a tent with friends
2. Review and self-evaluation	Chatting with friends after an event about how well the team performed, how well you did
3. Reviewing progress of others	Friends may ask you how well they have performed in activities
4. Setting targets for self and others	If you are in a sports team, aiming to improve your performance and team performance
5. Positive attitude to learning	Taking part in new activities, courses, skills etc.
6. Planning and preparation	Getting ready for school, going out with friends etc.
7. Customer care/dealing with clients	When you are in any sporting facility where there are other clients around
8. Timekeeping	Being on time for the bus, school, college, work etc.
9. Taking advice from others	Peers advising you about how you performed while taking part in a training session
10. Wearing appropriate dress	T-shirt for warm weather, jumper for cold weather, swimming costume for swimming etc.
11. Giving advice and feedback to others	When a friend asks your advice on something, e.g. clothes, music etc.
12. Awareness of health and safety issues	Walking across a road, walking on pavements instead of on the road, wearing a seatbelt in a car
13. Time management	Organising yourself in the morning before going to school, college, work etc.

Top Tip
The different colours (orange, green and blue) relate to what skills, qualifications and experience are contained within each career opportunity.

Top Tip
Employability skills are embedded within all of the Skills for Work courses. While you are carrying out the agreed tasks and duties, you will also be assessed against different employability skills.

Quick Test

1. What will different opportunities require you to have?

2. Why will each career opportunity have its own skills, qualifications and experience ?

3. What is incorporated into the Skills for Work course?

4. Do you use employability skills every day or just on the Skills for Work course?

Answers 1. Skills, experience and qualifications. **2.** Every opportunity will have its own set of industry requirements. **3.** Employability skills. **4.** Every day.

Employability skills and career pathways

Using employability skills

We have just looked at how you may be able to apply employability skills to other areas of your life – for example, going out with friends or taking part in team games. But how do employability skills relate directly with what you are doing on the Skills for Work course?

The table below shows examples of tasks and situations that each employability skill can be linked to while you are carrying out the tasks given to you by the person responsible in a sport and recreation facility.

Employability skill	How you may have used them on the Skills for Work course
1. Working co-operatively with others	When setting up and taking down equipment
2. Review and self-evaluation	After each Unit with the person responsible
3. Reviewing progress of others	During the 'Assisting with fitness programming' Unit
4. Setting targets for self and others	For my action plan and for client's training plan
5. Positive attitude to learning	I have demonstrated throughout the course
6. Planning and preparation	When I had to plan and prepare a component of an activity session
7. Customer care/dealing with clients	Whenever I was in the sports facility
8. Timekeeping	All the time while I was on the course
9. Taking advice from others	From the person responsible and senior colleagues
10. Wearing appropriate dress	When on activities and when cleaning and tidying facilities
11. Giving advice and feedback to others	During activity sessions
12. Awareness of health and safety issues	All the time while I carried out all Units of the course
13. Time management	When I was carrying out my work schedule in the facility

When you look at different career pathways, you can use your own employability-skill examples of how you were able to carry out agreed tasks, in order to build up a comprehensive picture of all the skills and experience you have gained throughout the Skills for Work course.

What skills, qualifications and experiences do I have?

By the time you have completed the Skills for Work course, you will have gained a number of skills, qualifications and experience. The best way to identify these attributes is to split them up into categories:

- Your education from school or college – give details about where you received your education, what subjects you took and what grade you gained (include the date of certification).

School and College info	Subjects taken	Result (grade)
The Best High School	English	2
	Skills for Work: Sport & Rec – Int 2	Pass
Top of the Hill College	NQ Leisure Industry & Sport Skills	Pass

- Other types of certificated qualifications – here you may wish to put any other assessments you have passed that you did not take at school, for example, first aid, pool lifeguard, community sports leader award etc.

Qualification name	Result	Date
1 day first aid	Pass	01/08/07
Pool Lifeguard	Pass	20/08/07

Top Tip
The person responsible should be able to inform you what employability skills are contained within each Unit and how these relate to the tasks you have to demonstrate for your assessment.

- Other types of qualifications, skills and experience (not certificated) – detail any courses that you have attended, but did not receive a certificate for. Courses that are not certificated may be 'in-house' training/assessment courses, or awareness courses (e.g. child protection etc.). Provide details of these courses and a brief explanation of what they were.

Details of skills, qualifications and experience	Explanation of course/experience
Specialist training on new gymnastics equipment	Rep from sports company came to show how to use a new piece of equipment the centre had bought
Child-protection workshop	Child-protection awareness training – ½ day

Top Tip
By compiling information about your skills, experience and qualifications, it is the first step to compiling your CV.

Quick Test

1. How could you achieve the employability skill 'Time management'?

2. How could you achieve the employability skill 'Reviewing progress of others'?

3. What category would a first-aid qualification be put under?

4. What are non-certified courses?

Answers 1. Carrying out my work schedule in the facility. 2. During the 'Assist with fitness programming' Unit. 3. Certified qualifications. 4. Courses that can be attended (e.g. in-house training) but are not certificated.

Assessing industry requirements

Career pathways

As you will be aware by now, the sport and recreation industry offers huge opportunities for anyone wishing to seek out employment. For your assessment of this Unit, you will have had to gain information on career or further-education opportunities from a range of resources, and get information on what skills, qualifications and experience are required for someone wanting to follow these pathways.

How will you know whether you are able to pursue a pathway? You will need to identify a minimum of two career pathways or jobs that you wish to pursue and mark off against the list of skills and qualifications that you have. Below is an example of this:

Job	Skills needed	Do I have these skills?
Leisure attendant	Customer-service skills	Yes, I have used all these skills on a Skills for Work course
	Setting up and taking down equipment	
	Cleaning and tidying	
	Safety checks	No
	Qualifications needed	Do I have these qualifications?
	Pool lifeguard	No
	First aid	Yes

Further education	Skills needed	Do I have these skills?
HNC/D Sports Coaching with Development of Sports	If candidates have relevant	Yes – these skills I have gained by being on a Skills for Work course
	experience – will be considered	
	Qualifications needed	Do I have these qualifications?
	NC Certificate or	Yes – these skills I have gained by being on a Skills for Work course
	2 x Higher Grades (or equivalent)	

How to identify my own strengths and weaknesses

At set times during the Skills for Work course, you will take part in reviews of the work and training sessions you have taken part in with the **person responsible**.

These reviews are designed to focus on all aspects of your course and your learning, in particular how you performed in your school or college work, what skills you have acquired, and what qualifications and experience you have gained.

Before you can identify what career pathway you wish to pursue, you need to find out what your strengths and weaknesses are. To identify your strengths and weaknesses, you will need to think back over all the occasions when you have been working with others in the sport and recreation environment while carrying out the tasks that were assigned to you by the person responsible – for example, interacting with customers, setting up equipment, assisting with activity sessions etc.

Sometimes it is easier to identify what your strengths and weaknesses are by making a note of them. You may get some ideas from your reviews with the person responsible and the employability-skills review. Do any of your strengths match any of your chosen career opportunities? Below are some examples:

My strengths	My weaknesses
I worked well with others when preparing for a session	I need to improve my timekeeping, as I was late arriving in the mornings
I was able to address most health-and-safety issues	I need to have more confidence in giving feedback to others

Top Tip
Find out where you would like to pursue a career in sport and recreation and make a list of the opportunities. You will need to narrow them down to two for your assessment!

Top Tip
When identifying your strengths and weaknesses, look over other reviews you have had with the person responsible in other Units.

Quick Test

1. What will you need to do for the assessment of this Unit?

2. How many career pathways will you need to identify as a minimum?

3. What will you need to find out before you can identify what career pathways you wish to pursue?

4. Where could you get ideas on what your strengths and weaknesses are?

Career plans and goals

Designing a career plan

In order to complete your career action plan, you will need to decide on what pathways you wish to follow. With the person responsible, you will decide on what further training, assessments experience and/or skills you will need in order to continue on these pathways, as this will help you to identify any development needs (further training) that you may need to take part in.

Your career action plan will be drawn up and based on:

- the information you have collected on your chosen career pathways, either from furthering your education (college/university/vocational qualifications etc.) or from looking at the different types of career opportunities there are, (i.e. leisure attendant, fitness instructor, outdoor instructor etc.)

- looking at what skills, qualifications and experience you have and what you will need to further your career in the sport and recreation industry, i.e. pool lifeguard, first aid etc.

- what your strengths and weaknesses are. This will influence what kind of career pathway you choose. For example, if you are a good swimmer, then gaining your pool life-guard qualification will be easy. However, if you have never been swimming before, this is a training issue that may need to be addressed if you wanted to become a pool lifeguard.

Reviewing a career plan

A review should take place on two separate occasions to monitor and review your progress. During your assessment, you will be progressing through the tasks set by the person responsible and ensuring that the assessment paperwork is fully completed.

On your first review with the person responsible, you will be asked to note up to five short-term and five long-term action points.

Examples of short-term action points

- gaining knowledge of industry requirements and/or further-education opportunities – this can be to research the requirements specific to a job or course

- finding out about courses that are being held, whether certificated or not. If they are crucial to your career pathway, then it may be important to attend these courses

- gaining real working experience to develop your skills in a working environment with the person responsible and other colleagues.

Examples of long-term action points

- looking at education progression routes into college, university, and vocational qualifications

- taking part in industry training and assessment courses.

The review process will also allow the person responsible to provide comments on the details of your short- and long-term action plans. The person responsible will also advise you on when these targets can be achieved.

To complete this Unit, you will have a second review with the person responsible to assess your progress from the first review. Comments will be made and targets revised on both the short- and the long-term action plans.

What further training will I need?

At both stages of your review with the person responsible, you will be having a look at your short- and long-term goals. During this time, you will identify what kind of further training you may need.

The career pathway you choose will determine the type of training you need to receive. The sport and recreation industry has a huge list of possible career pathways – for example:

1	Skills for Work – Sport and Recreation course	Gained basic skills and experience, and industry skills in the leisure, sport and outdoor industry
2	Get a job as a trainee or junior member of staff	Further experience and industry qualifications: acquiring the relevant skills for progression
3	Full-time member of staff; supervisor	Gaining higher industry-recognised qualifications and experience
	Centre manager	Training and development courses to progress into management

Top Tip

If you want to find out where career opportunities are near to you, it is best to look in local newspapers, or sport and recreation centres near to where you live, or along transport routes (bus or train) routes.

Quick Test

1. What two career opportunities are open to you?

2. When should your career-opportunity review take place?

3. Who will carry out your career-opportunity reviews?

4. Why may you need further training?

Adverts, letters and CVs

Job or career adverts

Career-opportunity information can be gained from a variety of sources, as mentioned before. Adverts for furthering your education can be found in:

- Newspapers
- Specialist industry magazines
- Television
- Looking at education websites/intranet sites

Fitness, Health and Exercise HND course
Start date: September. Entry requirements: two Highers or a NC in a sport and leisure subject.

Adverts for jobs can be very varied in their requirements. These kinds of adverts can be found in a variety of locations, for example, newspapers, websites/intranet sites etc. But all will give you information about what they are wanting from a potential employee. Here are some examples:

You have a great opportunity to work 16+ hours per week in a very friendly Women's only gym, limited weekends, no bank holidays and no late nights.

Basketball coaches required for the second week of June as a matter of urgency for a new contract we have been given in a school. We would only require Level 1 coaches but Level 2 can apply.

Learning and Leisure Services Instructor (37 hours)
You will be required to instruct school children in a range of outdoor and field study activities linked with a residential stay and additional equipment maintenance duties are expected at times through out the year. It is essential that you hold one of the following National Governing Awards:

Covering letters

Why do we need a letter that goes with our application form or curriculum vitae (CV)? The reason is that it is polite to send a letter to introduce yourself and give a few further details about the application form or CV that you have enclosed. The letter does not need to be an essay, but the hints opposite may be of use.

1. Ensure that you address your letter appropriately. There are ways you can ensure that you have addressed it correctly:

- if you <u>DO</u> know the name of the person the letter is to be sent to, then address your letter: e.g. Dear Mrs Wave

- if you <u>DO NOT</u> know the name of the person you are sending it to, then it is safe to put: Dear Sir or Madam.

2. Ensure that your letter is appropriate to what you are applying for. Include information relating to what you are applying for and a brief statement about yourself.

3. If at all possible, type your letter. This will ensure that it can be easily read by the person receiving it. It will also give the recipient a better impression of you!

4. To finish off your letter, the next thing you need to do is basically say "goodbye". The way this is done in letters is by using the following:

- If you have used "Dear Mrs Wave" at the beginning, you write "Yours sincerely".

- If you have used "Dear Sir or Madam" at the beginning, you write "Yours faithfully".

5. <u>DO NOT</u> forget to sign the letter!

Curriculum vitae (CV)

The term CV or curriculum vitae means "course of life" and is basically a record of who you are. It will sell your skills, qualifications and experiences and will paint a picture of you to a potential employer or course tutor. The person responsible will be able to take you through a step-by-step process on how to write a CV. Here are a few points:

- Ensure that it is tailored to what you are applying for – no point in sending off a CV for a sport and recreation course if its main focus is administration.

- Keep the CV simple, concise and easy to read – no-one wants to wade through long paragraphs of text.

- List your qualifications, employment history and experiences – these should be in chronological order, with the most recent at the top. Also give a brief explanation of what your duties or tasks were.

- Include personal information such as what your hobbies are.

- Include at least two references – these are people (referees) you will need to ask in advance. Referees will provide a **confidential** letter/statement about you to the organisation to which you have applied. This information will be directly related to what you have applied for.

Top Tip
Keep your CV up to date.

Top Tip
Make sure you keep copies of letters and CVs for future use.

Top Tip
When sending a covering letter, use good-quality paper. It will make your letter and attached application stand out against anyone else's.

Quick Test

1. Where can adverts for furthering your education be found?

2. If you are writing a covering letter, is it best to handwrite or type the letter out?

3. What do you finish off your letter with if you have addressed it "Dear Sir or Madam"?

4. What does CV mean?

Application forms and interviews

Application forms

When you apply for a job or a course, it is very important that you complete the application form they send you. The information they are requesting on their forms can be very specific to that company; however, some application forms may resemble the contents of your CV. Under **no** circumstances should you send in a CV as a substitute for an application form – it is a sign that you are lazy, and it will just end up in the bin! Unless the application form says otherwise, accompany your application form with your CV.

As with most of the content of the Skills for Work course, the **person responsible** will be able to assist you with how to complete an application form. Below are a few tips on completing an application form:

- DO read the instructions – most applications will have a list of instructions. For example, use only black ink, write only within specified spaces etc. Make sure you read through and refer to the instructions as you are completing the form.

- Photocopy the blank application form – this way, you can practise filling it in and then copy the correct information on to the original without making errors.

- Ensure that your writing is clear and legible – if it is, then the recipient will continue reading. If your writing cannot be read, then your application may be rejected.

- Enclosing other material – this could include references, your CV or extra information about yourself. Always read the instructions, whether you can enclose other material or not.

- Photocopy the completed application form – this will remind you what you have submitted before you attend your interview.

- Do not lie! If you elaborate on the truth (or lie), you will be found out, especially when you get to the interview. Do sell yourself, but keep the facts true.

  And lastly …

- Always keep the application form clean (no coffee-cup stains etc.).

- If you have to post off the application form, use an envelope that is large enough to fit the form, so that you don't have to fold it.

Interviews

Well done! You have managed to get an interview. What do you do now?

It is advisable that you take time to prepare yourself from the time you are informed of the interview until the day of the interview. Sometimes employers may send out an information pack which will give you a brief description of the organisation or course you have applied for. Prior to the interview day, use this opportunity to:

→ 1. Find out about the centre/company/organisation.

- Is it a sports centre, outdoor centre?
- What activities/facilities do they have?
- What kind of clients use the centre?

2. Find out more about the course you have applied for.

- Your attendance – full- or part-time?
- What kind of activities/sports will you be having to take part in?
- Will you need to pay for any aspect of the course?

3. In both the points above, re-read your application, CV and letter, just in case you are asked any questions relating to them.

On the day of the interview:

1. You need to make sure that you are dressed appropriately.

- Ensure that you are wearing smart, clean and ironed clothes, as this will give a good impression.
- Even if the interview is for a sport and recreation job or course, dress appropriately for the interview – i.e. do not wear shorts, sleeveless T-shirts etc, as this you may make a poor impression.

2. Leave home in plenty of time to avoid being late.

3. If asked any questions, answer briefly unless you are asked to give more details – this avoids you 'waffling'.

4. Think about body language – as mentioned earlier on page 75, this can also give the interviewer the impression of whether you want the job or college placement!

5. Selling yourself – be honest and give information about what you have done, for example, what skills, qualifications and experience you have.

Top Tip
Remember: first impressions last!

Top Tip
Practice filling in application forms by photocopying them before completing the original to avoid making mistakes.

Top Tip
If you need help in completing written application forms, the person responsible will be able to assist you or give you information on who can.

Top Tip
Prepare well for an interview, do your history, read through any documents they send you and look presentable on the day.

Quick Test

1. What might happen if you do not fill in an application form and send in a CV instead?

2. Why is it useful to photocopy the application form?

3. What three points are useful to do prior to your interview?

4. Why must you be honest about any information you give about yourself?

Answers 1. It may end up in the bin. **2.** To remind you what you have submitted before attending the interview. **3.** Find out about the centre/company/organisation, find out about the course you have applied for, re-read any documents you have submitted. **4.** Because otherwise you will get caught out!

Glossary

Absorbed Where the body has taken in a substance through the skin.

Accident Something that can happen unexpectedly at any time and that has the potential to cause harm – for example, grazed knee, cut finger and so on.

Confidential (Information which is) private an individual, cannot be made public without the individual giving consent.

Constructive Improving or promoting development – balancing up negative with positive alternatives

COSHH Control of Substances Hazardous to Health – a set of regulations to ensure the safety of people who have to deal with substances such as chemicals.

Data Protection Act (1998) This act ensures that companies comply with the provisions for the regulation of: processing of information to be held, obtained or disclosed about individuals.

Duty of care This is a legal obligation imposed on individuals and organisations, requiring that they exercise a reasonable standard of care while performing any acts that could potentially harm others.

Emergency An unforeseen incident, such as fire or theft, that needs immediate action.

Employability skills Important skills that you must demonstrate and which you are required to perform to pass the course. See page 9 for a list of all the employability skills.

Hazard Anything with the potential to cause harm – for example, water on a floor.

Hazardous substance Any solid, liquid or gas that can cause harm to your body.

Health and safety A set of rules and regulations that all centres, staff and users must abide by to ensure their safety.

Inappropriate language Words or phrases (such as swearing) that you should not use in the centre, especially when talking to customers and participants.

Induction A formal process where new members of staff or clients are shown around a centre. Health, safety and emergency facilities will also be included in an induction.

Ingested Where the body has swallowed a substance.

Inhaled Where the body has breathed in a substance.

Injected Where the body has taken in the substance directly, for example through a needle.

Manual Handling Operations Regulations A set of regulations to ensure that organisations train their staff in the correct ways to lift, lower, pull or push large, heavy and awkward objects, in order to minimise injury to staff and clients.

Medical assistance Doctors, paramedics, nurses and so on, who are trained medically and can give advanced care to casualties.

NABs National Assessment Banks – your assessment paperwork.

Negligence Failure to act on an occurrence that has a damaging effect on others. 'Negligence' is also a form of legal action which, in essence, amounts to a failure to take reasonable care. It is necessary to show that the situation was one where the common law of negligence imposed a duty, that the duty was broken, and that damage was caused by the breach of duty.

Person responsible This is a person who will have direct responsibility for you – for example, teacher, tutor, instructor, coach, assessor, trainer and so on.

PPE Personal Protective Equipment – the correct and relevant equipment that you must use and wear when carrying out certain tasks such as first aid, cleaning and tidying and so on.

Realistic working environment A place where you will carry out your assessments. For example, these facilities can be: leisure centres, fitness suites, outdoor centres and so on.

Report An account of something that has happened that is a centre requirement. Most incidences require a written report, i.e. an accident report form.

Risk assessment Careful examination of what could cause harm to people. This process will enable you to identify whether you have taken enough precautions or should do more to prevent harm to you or others using the facility.

Scenarios Small role-play situations that you will have to act out in a sport-and-recreation environment.

Unit specifications A document that contains information about what you have to do in order to pass your course.

Velocity In relation to speed: it refers to the measurement of distance travelled per unit of time.

Index